ALONG THE GREEN  KU-524-389
OF BRITAIN

J. H. B. Peel

ALONG THE GREEN
ROADS OF BRITAIN

DAVID & CHARLES
Newton Abbot   London   North Pomfret (Vt)

British Library Cataloguing in Publication Data

Peel, J. H. B.
  Along the green roads of Britain
  1. Great Britain—Description and travel—1971
  I. Title
  914.1′04857   DA632
  ISBN 0–7153–8327–2

First published by Cassell & Company Limited in 1976
Reprinted by David & Charles in 1982

Printed in Great Britain
by Redwood Burn Limited, Trowbridge, Wilts
for David & Charles (Publishers) Limited
Brunel House Newton Abbot Devon

Published in the United States of America
by David & Charles Inc
North Pomfret Vermont 05053 USA

*There is nothing at the end of any road
better than may be found beside it.*

EDWARD THOMAS

Contents

Illustrations

Kennet and Avon canal, Pewsey
Sugarloaf Mountain, Abergavenny
Ham Common on the Inkpen Ridgeway
Inkpen Church
The Inkpen Ridgeway, approaching River Hill
St Gennys Church, Cornwall
Farmhouse at St Gennys
Coombe Valley, Morwenstow
  E. W. Tattersall
Cliff path, near Bude
  E. W. Tattersall
Cornish Coast Path near St Gennys

All photographs, unless otherwise acknowledged,
are by the author

In the Beginning

1 In the Beginning

THE road lay like a green carpet through yellow corn. It was wide enough to take a tractor, yet so empty that the solitude could be seen a mile ahead, and so silent that only a chiff-chaff spoke, repeating an untranslatable proposition from the topmost branch of a September tree. No house appeared; not even the roof of a house. Fore-and-aft the broad belt of turf curved like a question-mark that had long ago given up hope of receiving an answer. Nor was the silence a mere interval. It was prolonged, perennial. Year after year, all round the calendar, by day and at night, I had walked this way, and on each occasion the way was empty. Who, then, had made it? And when? And why?

The Celts made it, several thousand years ago, as a route for livestock and merchandise. They made it by felling trees, skirting swamps, raising banks, shifting boulders. Following the Celts, the Romans used the way whenever it suited their purpose, incorporating parts of it into a military road. The Saxons used it, too, and after them the Normans and the Tudors and the Stuarts. Throughout the eighteenth and nineteenth centuries it served as a highway for cattle drovers. Even in 1945 it was used by cottagers walking to farms and villages beside the track. Then came the ubiquitous car and the habit of not walking beyond the garage. So, the road was now neglected and overgrown. In short, it resembled hundreds of other green roads which traverse Britain from Cornwall to Caithness. Many such roads had been pioneered by men who, although they could neither read nor write, were able to make earthen pots, to sharpen metal spears, to perform religious rites. Other roads were charted by tribes who spoke an early form of English, and could record their thoughts in writing. Others, again, appeared during the Crusades, or when the Tudor towns grew large enough to attract cattle-dealers from distant parts. In the eighteenth and nineteenth centuries a green road or towing-path was laid beside canals; in the twentieth century several green roads were created by clearing and widening ancient tracks and then linking them with new sectors, to form a long-distance route like the Pennine Way. A green road, therefore, is not necessarily a prehistoric road. Its width will vary, being sometimes sufficient to take a cart, and sometimes more than sufficient to take a lorry. Its length will likewise vary, crossing six counties, or spanning only three parishes.

By revealing cross-sections of time and space, the green roads enable a traveller to walk from prehistory into the present day. During these journeys he will discover how greatly the pattern of rural life has changed during the past fifty years. For example, a ploughman in the reign of William the Conqueror led much the same sort of life as did his remote descendants in the reign of Charles II. Similarly, a country gentleman in the year 1600 led much the same sort of life as did his great-grandfather in 1500, and his great-grandson in 1700. True, the medieval open fields gave way to the Augustan enclosures, and the fortified manor house gave way to the stately Georgian home; yet agriculture remained the largest single employer of labour, so that a cottager worked either on the land or in some capacity which served those who did so work; and he seldom ventured far beyond his market town. Changes occurred indeed, but without ever disrupting the tempo and ethos of rural life. From John Leland to W. H. Hudson, the great travellers did not find that their books had been outdated before they were published. Today, by contrast, a castle or a village may disappear almost overnight, and the elderly traveller confronts a generation for whom the Britain of his youth seems in many ways as remote as Lyonesse.

The journeys which we shall make do not explore the entire length of a green road; if they did, they would achieve only a supererogation of superficiality. Instead, we shall follow a part of each road, sometimes for fifteen miles, at other times for less than three. On the Icknield Way we follow the hidden footsteps of Celts over the Chiltern Hills in Buckinghamshire and Oxfordshire. We do the same on a ridgeway through Berkshire, where the sites of prehistoric burial chambers and the traces of Saxon ploughing will raise enough questions to enliven the solitude. In Sussex we follow Stane Street, a Roman road, passing a Roman villa. In Wiltshire we walk beside a canal, and through a tunnel, and into a forest. From the summit of the Sugarloaf Mountain in Monmouthshire we look down on larks singing in a Welsh valley. Along the Abbot's Way we sample the dourest tracts of Dartmoor. We reach Scotland, and the country of the Lords Marchers, and Cornwall's Atlantic coast; all the while recreating the past, reassessing the present, imagining the future; sometimes meeting the famous, sometimes greeting the obscure; lying in the sun, trudging through the snow, entering an inn, leaning on a bridge; inclined to be pleased, yet not disinclined to be critical.

The criticism shall start here and now, by defying a convention which requires us to speak of metres instead of yards, of litres instead of pints, of hectares instead of acres, of Cumbria instead of Westmorland. Though I admire Goethe, and delight in Ronsard, I will not follow their businesslike descendants into the Graeco-Roman jargon of a common market-place. For a thousand years the men of this kingdom have measured Time and Space in miles and inches, in midday and midnight. I will not rewrite Shakespeare for the convenience of foreign customers: 'We've heard the chimes at 24.00 hours, Master Shallow.' I was born an Englishman, and I shall die an Englishman, speaking my native language, not lisping the cosmopolitan Shibboleths of Mammon.

There remains a brief postscript, as follows: many people regard the green roads as ways of escape from urban routine. Such roads are indeed both rural and remote, yet none of them leads to Arcady. Mountains are as real as motorways;

shepherds are as real as salesmen; farms are as real as factories. Moreover, a farm and a shepherd and a mountain do at least supply the basic necessities of life, but no one can exist on a diet of visible cars and invisible exports. Human beings may, of course, evolve into creatures for whom vitamin pills and test-tube parenthood seem more natural than roast beef and romance. At present, however, men still bear a close resemblance to Adam, who, when he quit Eden, and came down to Earth, tilled the soil thereof, and moved leisurely, and discovered that the cost of living, though always painful, seldom varied much from year to year. In short, the green roads do *not* escape from reality. They enter the heart of it; the joy and the anguish, the war and the peace, the past and the present.

The Icknield Way

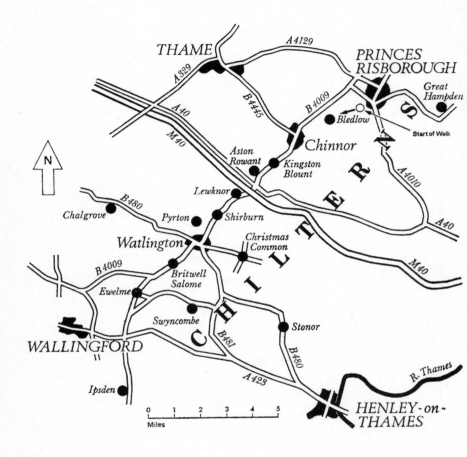

THAME

PRINCES
RISBOROUGH

A 4129

A 329

A 40

B 4445

B 4009

Great
Hampden

Bledlow

Start of Walk

M 40

Aston
Rowant

Kingston
Blount

Chinnor

C H I L T E R S

A 4010

A 40

B 480

Chalgrove

Pyrton

Lewknor

Shirburn

Watlington

Christmas
Common

M 40

B 4009

Britwell
Salome

Ewelme

Swyncombe

C H I L T

B 481

Stonor

B 480

WALLINGFORD

R. Thames

Ipsden

A 423

HENLEY-on-
THAMES

N

0   1   2   3   4   5
Miles

2 The Icknield Way

THE Icknield Way was a Celtic trade route from the east coast to the west country. Edward Thomas, who tried to trace the entire course, declared: 'The Icknield Way is sufficiently explained as the chief surviving road connecting East Anglia . . . with the west and the western half of the south of England.' Much of the Way has been so razed by tillage and building that its termini are unknown. The road probably began near the Gog Magog Hills in Cambridgeshire, and ended in Wiltshire. Thomas himself believed that it proceeded beyond Wiltshire. Indeed, he concluded his book by imagining that somebody might one day discover where the Way really did end: 'The utmost reward of this conjecturing traveller,' he suggested, 'would be to find himself on the banks of the Towy or beside the tomb of Giraldus at St David's.'

The most beautiful sector of the road crosses the Chiltern Hills between Bledlow in Buckinghamshire and Ewelme in Oxfordshire, where it divides into two parts, a Lower and an Upper, the latter having been used when rain flooded the valley route. About a mile south of Bledlow a lane crosses the Icknield Way, which at that point is itself a lane. Beyond the junction, however, the Way becomes a wide green road, and immediately starts to climb Wain Hill. I first saw this sector half a century ago, and for thirty-five years I lived within a few miles of it. Never a month passed without I walked there, at sunrise and after dark, through snow and in summer. The Chilterns are beautiful at all seasons, but in spring and autumn they surpass themselves, so that the October tints and the April leaves take even a native by surprise. I chose to travel in spring, during the first week of May, when the young foliage adds a gloss to Richard Jefferies' maxim: 'Beech and beautiful scenery go together.' Imagine, therefore, a green road climbing gently among beech trees, with hills ahead and hills astern, and on your right a vale whose destination is the horizon. Every leaf is tinged with silvery sunlight. Every vein on every leaf stands out, vivid as ebony. Birds flit across the Way, carrying food to their nests. During brief respites they sing from a bough ... blackbird, thrush, robin, wren, chiff-chaff, and spring's especial herald, the cuckoo. I once met a man who had tried three times to follow this sector, but never got above a quarter of a mile from the foot of Wain Hill; not because of the gradient, but because of the birds and the sun and the beeches. Having walked a few hundred yards, he became so enchanted that he sat down on a mossy bank, feeling that he was in Paradise, and need proceed no further.

My own progress did need to proceed further, not only in space but also through time, onward to Ewelme and backward to prehistory. Now the phrase 'prehistoric man' means 'all human beings who lived before writing was invented'. It is therefore a vague phrase, covering a span of nearly two million years. The word 'Celtic' is another vague term, which modern scholars define cautiously, to connote a people who occupied Europe north of the Alps, and were linked by cultural and linguistic ties. About the year 700 BC the Celts spread through a large part of western Europe, including Britain. Did they create the Icknield Way? It seems unlikely that any single tribe or generation pioneered an entirely new road across Britain. They would not have needed to do so. As the Romans exploited Celtic tracks, so the Celts exploited tracks that had been trodden by nomadic people seeking food and pastures. When the early inhabitants of Britain learned to make bronze about four thousand years ago, they became less primitive because the getting of food became less difficult, thereby allowing them to pursue other activities, notably trade, the *primum mobile* of organized transport. What we now call mass production can be traced to the Middle Bronze Age, when a new method of casting was devised, called *cire perdue* or lost wax, wherewith the craftsman made a beeswax model—of a cup, say, or an axe—which he coated with clay and then heated until the wax melted and the molten metal could be poured in. Thus, one man produced several objects from a single mould. Moreover, by discovering how to work sheet metal, the Bronze Age folk acquired cauldrons for boiling and preserving large quantities of food, a feat hitherto made impossible by lack of adequate vessels. The Bronze Age begat its own scrap merchants, the travelling tinkers, who collected old metal for melting.

Meanwhile, the Way began to climb more steeply, and entered a wood, where the trees had shed so many leaves through so many autumns that my footsteps sounded like a seaway. Whenever I halted, something stirred those leaves; either a squirrel pattering, or a bird hopping, or a beetle creeping. Having swerved right and left, the Way reached the summit of Wain Hill, eight hundred feet up, overlooking the Vale of Aylesbury, the distant Cotswolds, and the Warwickshire skyline. This was the road's highest point, from which Rupert Brooke surveyed 'the slumbering Midland plain'. Brooke, in fact, stayed several times at the Pink and Lily, a hilltop inn near Lacey Green, three miles north-west of the Way, where he wrote an autumnal evocation :

> White mist about the black hedgerows,
> The slumbering Midland plain,
> The silence where the clover grows,
> And the dead leaves in the lane . . .

Eastward the Chilterns stretched from the Thames at Great Marlow to the heights above Chequers Court at Ellesborough. On their slopes I saw Whiteleaf Cross, eighty feet wide, carved in the chalk. Tradition says that the Cross was made by Saxons to commemorate a victory over the Danes, but scholarship says that the Cross was made by Englishmen during the seventeenth century, for a purpose now unknown. There, too, stood Cymbeline's Mount or Castle, where excavation yielded oyster shells and a boar's tooth. Ellesborough men will tell you that the Mount marks the site of a battle between the Celtic chief and the Roman army. In 1695, however, Bishop Kennet stated that the battle took place far to the north of Ellesborough: 'The Romans,' he asserted, 'marcht towards a river, on the other side of which the Britons were encampt ... This action seems to have been on the river Ous near Buckingham.' So far as I can discover, Cymbeline died before any Roman army reached the River Ouse.

On the summit of Wain Hill stands a brick-and-flint cottage, a comely example of Chiltern domestic architecture, now fallen from fashion because breeze-blocks are cheaper than local flints. Passing within a few feet of it, the Way turns south-west along the edge of Bledlow Great Wood and thence downhill. At this point the grass had been churned by horsemen, but it soon recovered, and presently crossed a lane from Chinnor, less than half a mile away, which used to be a quiet village with many thatched and timbered houses. Today it is a loud eyesore, dominated by Chinnor Cement Works, whose chimneys can be seen afar off, fouling the air with smoke. Beyond Chinnor the Way curved south-west, and became wide again, following level ground at the foot of hilltop woods: Crowell Hill Wood, Kingston Wood, Grove Wood, Ashton Wood. It was woods all the way, so lofty that I needed to peer up at them, yet so near that I could have reached them by crossing a couple of fields. A stranger might describe the scene as unpeopled, but a native would glimpse the roofs of three hamlets, each within a mile of its neighbours. First came Crowell, the place where crows haunted an *aewielm* or brook; next, Kingston Blount, a royal manor, which in 1279 was held by a blond Norman, Hugo de Blund; finally, Aston Rowant, which in 1236 was held by another Norman, Rowald de Eastun, lord of the *tun* or settlement eastwards from Lewknor. Grass and corn lapped the southern side of the Way, which was now wide enough to take a brace of lorries. Southward the beechwoods streamed like a green banner on a blue breeze, recalling Defoe's amazement at their profusion: 'Beech ... the quantity of this, brought from hence, is almost incredible, and yet is the country so overgrown with beech in those parts, that it is brought very reasonable, nor is there like to be any scarcity of it for time to come.'

I now glanced over my shoulder, as though expecting to be joined by a friend. Sure enough, the friend arrived, or rather the ghost of a friend, for Time had overtaken the single-line railway between Princes Risborough and Watlington. The rails had gone; the signals had gone; the halts had gone. Only the course remained, running within a few feet of the Way, like one green road greeting another. How strange, I thought, that a prehistoric track should have outlived a Victorian track; how confounded, the nineteenth-century journalist who predicted: 'Steam has outstripped even the fastest Mail coach. Railways, the wonder of our Age, have begun a journey of infinite length. It is impossible to imagine that they will ever be outpaced by some new mode of travel. What would our grandfathers have said, could they see us hurtling through the English countryside at five-and-twenty miles an hour?' The Watlington train hurtled through the English countryside at five-and-thirty miles an hour; a Great Western tank engine and two small coaches. If the guard sighted a passenger hurrying to catch the train at Wain Hill halt, he obligingly delayed his departure therefrom, and then strolled up to the driver, to discuss whatever happened to be the topic for the day. Both men spoke the Chiltern dialect, with its drawling vowels and an inability to pronounce 'I' except as 'Oi'. Sometimes they talked of politics, often of the weather, occasionally of women: 'Oi told 'er straight ... "When oi married you," oi said ... but arter thart oi couldn't git a bloody word in. Oi 'ad to laugh, though, 'cause when we was courting oi used often to say to 'er,

"You're a quiet 'un, my gal." ' At that moment the belated
passenger arrived, clutching a shopping basket; whereupon
the guard waved, the driver whistled, and Time puffed on,
through cornfields at the foot of beechwoods, with a cargo of
wire netting, empty milk churns, weekly newspapers, three
pigs, and eleven passengers.

For nearly a mile the Victorian track kept pace with the
Celtic track, and was twice crossed by lanes linking the
Upper with the Lower Icknield Way; the latter being a
metalled lane. At one of those crossings stood a railwayman's
hut, whose design and materials were a legacy of Britons
riding the crest of a wave, from which, since they foresaw no trough, they wrought confidently, conscientiously,
and with a courteous effort to please the eye. The road
itself was now wider than any of the neighbouring lanes.
The larks were loud, the sun stood high, and I strode in
rhythm with the 'Rondeau' from Mozart's rollicking Horn
Concerto.

Near Warren Farm the old railway forsook the old highway, heading westward for Lewknor, there to haunt those
elderly villagers who in their youth had regarded it as a link
with Buckingham Palace, Madame Tussaud's, and the
Tower of London. By this time I was in Oxfordshire, having
walked five miles without seeing or hearing anyone. Such
solitude would have astounded Edward Thomas : 'Where the
Icknield Way through Buckinghamshire rounds the promon-
tory Beacon of the Ivinghoe Hills,' he wrote, 'I have seen
men with sheep from Berkshire to Dorset journeying towards
Dunstable, Royston, and the farms of Cambridgeshire and
Suffolk.' That, by the way, was written during my own lifetime. Even in the 1950s many gipsies camped along the Way,
squatting beside a fire while their linen dried on a hedgerow.
Some of the nomads slept in a horsedrawn caravan; others
pitched tents; a few bedded down under a tattered awning,
slung from the branch of 'a tree. Borrow's gipsy, you remember, would gladly have lived for ever with the wind on the
heath. Alas, the wind on the heath has given way to the walls

of a compound. Few gipsies now live like Shakespeare's duke: 'He is already in the forest of Arden, and many a merry man with him ... and fleet the time carelessly, as they did in the golden world.' If anyone tells you that gipsies are far better off in a home, depend upon it that he never walked the Icknield Way fifty years ago, when gipsies sang and smoked and smiled, and never more heartily than when the rain poured down. Neither education nor sanitation is a synonym for *joie de vivre*.

When the road became less wide I began to listen for a disagreeable sound. After a few minutes I heard it and finally saw it, because the grass ended abruptly at the main highway between Oxford and London, where all repose and dignity disappeared beneath vehicles speeding like compulsive ants. On the far side of the race-track I could see the green road proceeding as though nothing had happened. The dog and I waited, hoping that one at least of the vehicles would remember that pedestrians take precedence on the Queen's highway. When it became obvious that the maniacs never would yield, I picked up the dog, sprinted through a gap in the traffic, and rejoined the Way, which now assumed a Romanesque straightness. After a while the stench and the roar receded, and were replaced by birdsong and the scent of hawthorn. On the left stood more hills: Beacon Hill, Bald Hill, Shirburn Hill, Pyrton Hill, Watlington Hill. They stretched as far as I could see, and all their crests were wooded: Hailey Wood, Cowleaze Wood, and (someone having run short of ideas) Beechwood. They shone, those woods. Their leaves shone; their boles shone; their undergrowth shone; and the bare slopes of them shone, green-grassed or emerald-grained. As for the race-track, it soon afterwards became a motorway with fly-overs and speed-unders. And there the green Icknield Way makes the ghastliest of all its crossings. There is, however, another ghastly encounter a few miles north of Royston in Hertfordshire, where the main road sheers away to the left while a short sector of the green Way keeps straight on. In 1976 the first twenty yards of that grass were fouled by motorists and lorry drivers who used it as a public lavatory and rubbish dump.

Having shaken off the ghost of a railway, I became aware of the ghost of a man, Edward Thomas, who wrote *The Icknield Way*. Concerning his own progress through life, Thomas said: 'And I rose up, and knew that I was tired, and continued my journey.' The story of Edward Thomas deserves to be sketched, partly because it is a feature of the Way and partly because it illustrates the plight of an artist in society. Thomas was born at Lambeth, in 1878, son of a minor civil servant. While still an undergraduate of Lincoln College, Oxford, he married, and within a few years found himself with a family of four. Society in general and his father in particular urged him to obtain regular employment. Thomas, however, was an artist. As a very young man he had published some lyrical essays, chiefly about the countryside; but such wares never have been profitable. He therefore supported his family by reviewing books and by producing a spate of guides, anthologies, and 'popular' biographies. At one time he was writing a full-length book for less than £38. In 1913, when his life had become almost unbearable, he met Robert Frost—then an unknown American poet—who soon perceived what Thomas himself had failed even to guess, that the pot-boiler concealed a poet. Encouraged by his new friend, Thomas began to write verse, not only about the countryside but also about love, ambition, age, and death. He was then nearer forty than thirty years old, and to his friend Eleanor Farjeon he remarked wryly: 'Did anyone ever begin at thirty-six in the shade?'

My thoughts were suddenly interrupted by the sight of an old man and his dog, resting beside a field-gate.

'Lovely morning,' I remarked.

'Treat to be aloive,' came the reply.

'Walking far?'

'Thart depends on wart you mean by far. When oi were a young charp oi didn't reckon as oi'd started to walk, not until oi'd covered a dozen moile. And arter oi'd done twenty oi always made a point o' resting in case th' old dog were puffed. But nowadays,' he ran a hand down his spine, 'nowadays oi can't manage no more nor a moile, and even then oi gits thart slow, the bloody snails overtake me. How far can *you* manage?'

'Not so far as I used.'

'We all come to it one day. Thart is, if we live long enough.' His eyes twinkled. 'Oi can still breathe, though.'

He went on to tell me that he had been born within three miles of the Way. 'Weather permitting,' he added, 'oi takes a stroll 'ere twoice a week. My granddaughter,' he nodded towards a lane which crossed the Way, four hundred yards ahead, 'she koindly droives me 'ere. T'ain't more nor ten minutes from where oi live. Makes a noice level stroll, th'old Icknield.'

We walked slowly while the past came to life.

'Oi'd a huncle once—gentleman by the name o' James Gurney—and thart old fella was so fond o' loife he didn't pack it in till he were noinety-six, which is tickling along as you moight say. Anyow, when J. Gurney were a boy he saw 'undreds o' sheep travelling this road. The drovers used to make an arrangement with the farmers so's their flocks could spend the noight in a meadow. Thart's why some places are still called Penny Field and Farthing Patch. Any'ow, when my grandma were a little 'un the pedlars travelled this road, too, carrying ribbons and needles and suchloike.'

As we approached the lane, the veteran halted. 'Ah well, there's my granddaughter. Oi can 'ear the car radio. Thart's summat you and me was spared when we were 'er age.' He raised his stick in farewell. 'Have a noice walk.'

I did have a nice walk, quite forgetting Edward Thomas while I tried to imagine the Way as it had appeared to the Celts who inhabited a wooded wilderness teeming with wolves and bears and boars. Since the population of Britain was then less than that of modern Manchester, it is difficult to conceive the loneliness of those early travellers walking from Cambridgeshire to Wiltshire, day and night on guard against wild animals and hostile strangers. The suffering of such people numbs the imagination. Few of them lived to be forty; all were haunted by fantasies and superstitious delusions. They went in dread of drought, famine, flood. Their existence was little more than a monotonous search for food and shelter. If they could return to the Icknield Way now, they would stare amazed at the trim hedges and fertile fields; at sheep and cattle so plump that they made the Celtic stock look like stunted hybrids; and at the green road itself, no longer a highway for barefoot nomads, but a neglected track, visited twice a week by an old man and his dog, and occasionally by farmhands working in the fields.

Crossing one of those fields, I made a mile-long detour to the village of Shirburn, whose medieval name, *Scireburn*, meant 'bright stream', a reference to one of several which flowed northward into Haseley Brook. Standing in a park near the church, Shirburn's towered and moated castle was built by Warren de L'Isle during the fourteenth century. One of its eighteenth-century lords, the Earl of Macclesfield, began his career as the son of a Staffordshire lawyer, and ended it as Lord High Chancellor of England. Like an earlier chancellor, Francis Bacon, the earl was found guilty of corruption. After a period in the Tower he forsook public life and reappeared only once, as a pall-bearer at Sir Isaac Newton's funeral. The next Lord Macclesfield was an eminent astronomer, who employed at his observatory two workers from the Shirburn estate : John Bartlett, a shepherd, and Thomas Phelps, a stableman. So well did the earl instruct his assistants, and so lively were their talents, that each became a reliable observer, and one of them had a paper published by the Royal Society.

From Shirburn I could not resist crossing a few more fields to the hamlet of Pyrton, seeking the ghost of yet another wayside personage, John Hampden, whom Lord Clarendon likened to Cinna: 'He had a head to contrive, a tongue to persuade, and a hand to execute any mischief.'

Hampden was a rich landowner, whose ancestors had held Great Hampden since before the Norman Conquest. Despite his riches, or perhaps because of them, Hampden joined the rebels, hoping to increase the power of the gentry by decreasing the prerogative of the King. At Pyrton he married Elizabeth Symeon, daughter of the lord of that manor, whose Tudor home remains intact. When Elizabeth died prematurely, Hampden remarried. Some years later, in 1643, Prince Rupert rode out from Oxford, intending to attack the rebels, whom he met at Chalgrove Field, only a few miles from Pyrton. Hampden took part in the battle. According to Clarendon, he was 'shot into the shoulder with a brace of bullets, which brake his bone....' The wounded man rode away, seeking shelter at his first wife's home. In order to get there he had to jump his horse across Haseley Brook. Already weak from loss of blood, he found the effort too much, and therefore made his way to Thame, where he died some days later, at the house of an apothecary.. Hampden's retirement from the battle dismayed the rebels. Clarendon, in fact, said that it caused 'as great a consternation of all that party, as if their whole army had been defeated, or cut off'. Of Hampden's death, however, he remarked only that it was 'a great deliverance to the nation'. The dead man was buried at Hampden House (now a girls' school), attended by soldiers from the regiment which he had recruited and equipped, the Buckinghamshire Greencoats. Two centuries afterwards a grisly postscript was written by Lord Nugent, the Whig historian, who, wishing to discover the manner of Hampden's death, whether by enemy action or by a defective pistol, obtained permission to exhume the body, which was done late at night, but without solving the problem. During the years when I lived almost within sight of Great Hampden House, the rector told me that Lord Nugent had probably opened the wrong coffin.

The clock was striking two when I left Pyrton. However, a tradesman drove me back to the Icknield Way, enabling me to rejoin my route only a few hundred yards from where I

had left it. Looking about for somewhere to rest, I found it
under a bank. Now of all the objects on which men have
reclined, none is more comfortable than a well-grooved
grassy bank that has been dried by sun and wind. So there
I lay, full length on the turf, with my head supported by a
pillow of primroses; and in that luxury I forgot the past,
dismissed the future, and allowed the present to seep through
the pores and thence into the brain, or the intellect, or the
soul, or whatever else you care to call that part of us which
appears to be the seat of self-consciousness. I certainly became conscious of a cardinal difference between the earliest
and the latest Britons; for whereas the former lived chiefly
out of doors, indulging a deep empathy with their environment, the latter lived chiefly indoors, and many of them
could not tell cabbage from kale. Edward Thomas, by contrast, did indulge a deep empathy with his environment, but
in *The Icknield Way* he was too weary to say so. One of his
biographers, Robert Eckert, rated the book as 'the weariest
of Thomas's ... and the dullest'. Thomas, in fact, had ex-
hausted himself with prose, but had not yet discovered himself in poetry. His journey along the Way lasted about ten
days. He rose each morning before six, and on one occasion
became so footsore that he had to rest and then walk thirty
miles next day, making up for lost time. He travelled hatless,
wearing a soiled raincoat. Sometimes he did not shave. He
was defeated before he started, and he confessed as much in
the dedication to his friend, Harry Hooton: 'This book for
you was to have been a country book, but I see that it has
turned out to be another of those books made out of books
founded on other men's books.'

Undertaken not for love but for money, Thomas's journey
became a tedious duty. He passed through Whiteleaf without saying something of its famous Cross. He passed through
Ewelme without mentioning its chief glories, the tomb of the
Duchess of Suffolk, and the almshouses which she and her
husband founded. When he did reveal himself, it was in ways

so misplaced that one marvels at the publisher's acceptance of them; for example: 'I am weary of everything. I stay because I am too weak to go on. I crawl on because it is easier than to stop. I am not a part of nature. I am alone. There is nothing else in my world but my dead heart and brain.' Suffering had blunted his critical insight, which knew very well that self-pity, no matter how poignant, is not a fit subject for the kind of book he was writing.

Meanwhile, the angle of the sun advised me to continue my own journey, so I left the mossy bank, following a Way which became rather narrow, though still wider than a foot-path. At a place called White Mark I sighted the distant roofs of Watlington, which Edward Thomas described as 'a big square village of no great beauty'. Chilternfolk, on the other hand, regard Watlington as a town; and to me its beauty is self-evident. Six narrow streets converge beside a seventeenth-century market hall of warm red brick, supported by vaulted arches. Some of the houses are Georgian and therefore handsome. Watlington was the Saxon *tun* or settlement of *Wacol*'s tribe. William the Conqueror granted the manor to Robert d'Oilli, whence it passed to the Earl of Norfolk, who received the King's permission to hold a weekly market there. They say that John Hampden slept at Watlington, on the eve of Chalgrove Field, at an inn which has vanished. Edward Thomas certainly slept there, at an inn which has not vanished. For supper and a bed he paid (in our own currency) ten pence. Breakfast he did not pay for, because he was up and away by five o'clock next morning. I, too, slept at Watlington, at the same inn. For supper, bed, and breakfast I paid the equivalent of thirty not-so-new pence. That was in 1929.

Another mile brought me to a point which the Ordnance map marked as Icknield, a mysterious name. In AD 913 the Way was called *Icenhilde Weg*; in 1185 traces of a Roman name were preserved as *Ikenhildstrate*; but the meaning of 'Icknield' remains unknown and a source of error. Thus, Ickleford in Cambridgeshire, and Ickleton in Hertfordshire, both stand on the Icknield Way, yet neither was named after it; Ickleton being the *tun* of *Icel*'s tribe; Ickleford, the ford of *Icel*'s tribe. Antiquaries used to believe that the Way was named after an East Anglian tribe, the Iceni, whose leader, Queen Boudicca, defied the Romans; but scholars now question the belief. In 1677 Robert Plot's *Natural History of Oxfordshire* emphasized the loneliness of the Way, its undoubted association with brigands, and its alleged association with the Iceni: 'it passes through no town or village in the County, but only Goreing; nor does it (as I hear) scarce any where else, for which reason 'tis much used by stealers of Cattle ... it seems by its pointing to come from Norfolk and Suffolk, formerly the Kingdom of the Icnehild or Ikenhild ...' A century later, Hearne's *Journal* showed that the name had been corrupted: 'I went thro' Ewelme ... and about 2 furlongs east said Ewelme passeth the *lower Hackneywaye* ...' Hearne's contemporary, William Stukeley, decided that the Way was a Roman road: 'the great Icening street of the Romans.' Isaac Taylor, the philologist, survived into the twentieth century, yet his *Words and Places* added vagueness to confusion by stating: 'Icknield Street led from Norwich to Dorchester and Exeter.' One assumes that Taylor's 'Street' is the Icknield Way; but no one has yet proved that it led from Norwich to Exeter via Dorchester. Edward Thomas collated the various hypotheses about the Way's name and route, but accepted none of them: 'The theorists and conjecturers,' he wrote, 'have done little to ascertain the course of a road which can safely be called the Icknield Way.' By whatever name, the Way was one of four roads—Ermine Street, Foss Way, and Watling Street being the others—which received from William the Conqueror the privilege of the King's Peace for the protection of travellers. A Norman chronicler congratulated William on the safety of his roads: 'A man of any class might travel throughout the kingdom unhurt with his bosom full of gold.' The Chilterns, however, continued as a hive of outlaws seeking shelter in the woods and combes. The Normans therefore instituted the Stewardship of the Chiltern Hundreds—that is, of Stoke, Desborough, and Burnham—to act as a police force. The stewards were required also to collect certain payments on behalf of the Crown, from which they amassed a sizeable fortune. Despite these precautions, the Chilterns continued to attract criminals. When Dante's tutor visited Shirburn Castle he was waylaid by robbers, and had to run for his life. In time, of course, the Hills lost their evil reputation, and by the middle of the eighteenth century the stewardship had become a sinecure. Why, then, do members of the House of Commons sometimes apply for it? The answer is to be found in two Statutes; one of 1623, which forbade members to resign their seats unless for grave and urgent reasons; the other of 1707, which forbade members to accept an 'office of profit under the Crown'. The former Statute was passed because members tended to resign in order to look after their private affairs; the latter, because the Crown tended to bribe members by offering lucrative posts outside the Commons. In 1750, at all events, a member wished to resign his seat and to stand for another constituency. Looking about for an 'office of profit under the Crown', he chose the Stewardship of the Chiltern Hundreds, which is now the customary excuse for resigning from the Lower House.

At Icknield the Way was still a green road, but having crossed the lane from Watlington to Stonor it became a footpath, overhung by trees and hedgerows. Soon it passed a secluded farm near Howe Wood, which the Ordnance map marked as Dame Lys, though from time immemorial it has been called Dame Alice, and is still so called by natives who remember that Alice Chaucer (a granddaughter of the poet) was lady of the nearby manor of Ewelme. Her father, Thomas Chaucer, Speaker of the House of Commons, acquired Ewelme by marriage. Dying in 1434, he left one child, Alice, who, when she was about twelve years old, married Sir John Philips, but was widowed when he fell during the siege of Harfleur. Within a short while the child married the Earl of Salisbury, and was again widowed when he fell at the siege of Orleans. Her third husband was William de la Pole, Marquess of Suffolk, with whom she travelled to France, to bring back Margaret of Anjou for her marriage with Henry VI. Having been created a duke, William was murdered by his rivals, whereupon the dowager duchess sought safety at her manors in Oxfordshire and Norfolk. In 1469 Margaret Paston reported: 'The Duchess of Suffolk is at Ewelme in Oxfordshire ... that she might be far out of the way, and rather feign excuses because of age or sickness if that the King would send for her.' The King did send for her, not to threaten, but to appoint her as custodian of the widowed Queen whom she had once escorted from France, the troubled and troublesome Margaret of Anjou, now a prisoner of Edward IV. Margaret Paston then informed her son: 'As for Queen Margaret, I understand that she is removed from Windsor to Wallingford, nigh to Ewelme, my lady Suffolk's place.' Tradition says that the Queen was moved from Wallingford to the duchess's manor at Ewelme, which incorporated fragments of the old Palace of Ewelme. Leland described the Palace as 'within a fair moat and builded richly of brick and stone'. Half a century later, when James I became King of England, the Palace was decaying.

Beyond Dame Alice Farm the road became so overgrown that I had to duck between the branches. Unlike the Romans, who would have dismissed it as a typical barbarian track, the eighteenth-century English would have accepted it as a typical country lane. In 1723, for example, Lord Harley complained that parts of the road from London to Canterbury were too narrow for horsemen to ride abreast 'or even as much as two wheelbarrows'. Although medieval law required that two hundred feet of ground be kept clear on each side of the highway, as a precaution against robbers, many landowners either enclosed the ground for cultivation or allowed the undergrowth to spread unchecked. In 1652 John Evelyn warned travellers not 'to ride neere an hedge'. Some of Evelyn's friends sent a footman ahead, armed with an axe, to clear a passage for their coach. More than two hundred and fifty years later, in 1912, parts of the main road across Shap Fell in Westmorland were so bad that motor-cyclists sometimes fractured the frame of their machines while bumping over pot-holes.

In sunny places the Way was covered with leaves that shone like russet pools rising from a spring of unfathomable autumns. Flitting through shafts of light, a bullfinch mimed a moving rainbow. By stirring the undergrowth with my stick I uncovered several primroses, yellow-stemmed and stunted. The Chiltern sector of the Way is well endowed with flora and fauna. Oxfordshire, in fact, has 242 species of birds, of which 60 are resident, 71 are migrant, and 111 are occasional visitors. Seldom heard elsewhere in the southern counties, stone curlews and cirl buntings are resident in the Chilterns, while stonechats and wheatears return each year. Some of the old people still use such traditional nicknames as gizer or missel-thrush, and hickle or green woodpecker (also dubbed hickwall and hickway). On the slopes of Watlington Hill I noticed many junipers. Higher yet, at the lovely-sounding hamlet of Christmas Common, were spindle trees, dwarf orchis, and autumn gentian. Had I ventured south a few miles, to Peppard and Ipsden, I would have found heather. As it was, I sighted some vivid patches among the hilltop woods, where bluebells surged like a static sea; and everywhere the chalk slopes abounded in chicory.

The overgrown sector soon ended, and the Way once more became a wide green road at the foot of wooded hills, but nowhere did it reveal anyone tilling the soil. Formerly a gregarious occupation, agriculture is now a synonym for solitude. A man may plough all day without seeing or hearing another human being. Yet in his grandfather's time several teams ploughed alongside, and mowers and harvesters worked in long lines, singing and talking, and at noon eating together. 'Poetry,' said Edward Thomas, 'is better than prose.' Being by trade a poet, I did my best to evoke the empty landscape, memorizing the words while I walked:

> The land is lonely now;
> A tractor-man can plough
> More furrows in one hour
> Than any horse-hauled power.
> He rides alone, where formerly there walked
> Three jingling teams abreast, that sang and talked.
>
> The haytime is a swift
> And reeking roar; no drift
> Of badinage while scythes
> Sweep swathes through hills and hythes.
> The task of twenty mowers now employs
> Two witless tractors and two wordless boys.
>
> Over a stubbled loam
> The harvest hurries home
> To television; all
> The coloured carnival
> Has gone, and all the merriment that led
> To man's thanksgiving for his daily bread.
>
> Now the land is lonely,
> Reaped and tilled by only
> A remnant of the folk
> Who bore its heavy yoke,
> Beneath whose weight they often rose, with health
> And cheerfulness of heart, their richest wealth.

Skirting North Farm, the Way turned from south-west to north-west, and for nearly a mile kept so close to the woods that I heard squirrels pattering through leaves. These changes of direction achieved a compromise between a Roman straightness and a Chestertonian deviousness ('that night we went to Birmingham by way of Beachy Head'). In short, the Way followed the wisdom of the ages, going more or less straight when the country was level, and more or less crooked when the country was steep; a custom that pleased Edward Thomas: 'The straight road,' he believed, 'can only be made by those in whom extreme haste and forethought have destroyed the power of joy, either at the end or any part of its course.' Straight or crooked, a green road is both a balm for sore feet and a spur for swift limbs. No other walkable surface vies with turf; witness the speed of a cricket ball on a fast outfield. True, the turf becomes soft after prolonged rain, and hard after prolonged drought, but in equable weather it remains unbeatable. Hazlitt summed it up when he said: 'Give me the clear blue sky over my head, and the green turf beneath my feet, a winding road before me.'

Before me on my own winding road stood a distant sky-line, crowned by Wittenham Clumps alias Dorchester Clumps alias Berkshire Bubs alias Sinodun Hills. There are, in fact, two clumps of trees, marking the site of an Iron Age fort which the Romans enclosed (one of their altars was found nearby). In 1782 a German pastor, Carl Philip Moritz, climbed that hill, and was puzzled 'by what appeared to be the mast of a ship, standing up from behind it ... When I reached the summit, however, I found that the mast was stuck in the ground to entice the curious from the road.' Having returned to the foot of the hill, Moritz noticed 'a house with many people looking out of the window and apparently laughing at me'. Little minds always have been pleased by childish things. In the end, however, the German visitor was enchanted by this part of the Chilterns. At the village of Nettlebed, near Chalgrove Field, he was so hospitably received that he could hardly bear to say goodbye: 'Three times I started to leave it to continue my walk, and each time I was drawn back to it, on the verge of resolving to stay there a week or longer.' In 1929 I, too, was hospitably received at Nettlebed, by the proprietor of the same inn that had befriended Pastor Moritz.

The Way at this point crossed a wide belt of grass with high woods on the left, and a pastoral plain on the right, stretching as far as Oxford. The horizon shimmered in the afternoon heat, but the birds were still loud, and a stray breeze rustled the leaves. The rest was silence, sunshine, solitude. Away to the right I could just see the roofs of Britwell Salome, anciently called *Britewelle Solham* or 'place with a bright stream', whose lord in 1236 was *Aumaricus de Suleham* (the *ham* or 'settlement' in a *sulh* or 'narrow valley'). Edward Thomas took little notice of the village: 'Britwell Salome church,' he remarked, 'lay on my right, across a willowy field ...' Had he explored Britwell he would have found a courtly manor house and a rebuilt Norman church containing sixteenth-century brasses, seventeenth-century woodwork, and an eighteenth-century gallery. But Thomas was in no mood to explore. Instead, he marched wearily on, to the last of all his journeys. Declining Frost's invitation to migrate to America, where he could have avoided the war, he became a subaltern in the Royal Garrison Artillery, still writing the poems which he never lived to see published. He was killed in action on Easter Sunday 1917, having practised his own preaching: 'Poetry is better than prose.' Some writers outlive their fame, but Thomas died while his own was being born, before the sap began to fail, or the fashion to change, or the world to forget. In one of his last poems, *The Trumpet*—scribbled on a sheet of artillery calculations—he sounded both a private and a universal Reveille which raised him to his rightful place among the English poets:

> Open your eyes to the air
> That has washed the eyes of the stars
> Through all the dewy night;
> Up with the light,
> To the old wars;
> Arise, arise!

Meanwhile the afternoon wore on, seeming more like summer than spring. The buttercups glistened, the beech-boles gleamed, and among them another patch of bluebells outshone the lakes that are painted on maps. Truly the Chilterns flaunted their Sunday-best; green and gold, blue and pink, yellow and white; cattle in meadows, and sheep beside streams; acres of corn, centuries of woods, harmonies of birds. The beeches still climbed on the left; the vale still shimmered on the right; the villages still kept their distance. But now at last I was nearing journey's end. Indeed, I could see it, three hundred yards ahead, where the green road joined a metalled lane from Ewelme to Swyncombe via Sliding Hill, a name worthy of the practical poets who coined it. If you have ever ventured on Sliding Hill during frosty weather you will readily believe that a Chiltern peasant one day entered the tavern at Ewelme, rubbing his backside ruefully, and saying: 'Oi didn't 'alf come a cropper on thart 'ill. T'aint fit for marn nor beast this weather. Next toime oi goes to Swyncombe oi'll stick to the bloody fields.' His neighbours, no doubt, kept the incident alive by asking: 'Done any more sloiding on th'ole 'ill?' And that, perhaps, is how Sliding Hill received its name.

The hill itself is a semi-circular escarpment topped by beech trees, with woods on the left, and fields on the right, chiefly of roots and corn. Before proceeding into Ewelme, I climbed Sliding Hill for old times' sake, en route for Swyncombe. In 1086 the village was called *Svincumbe* or 'pig valley'. As I climbed the hill, I noticed upward of twenty pigs grubbing in a field. Partway up the hill, a farm and a cottage looked across the fields and thence to the furthest corner of the escarpment. Each house was built of brick and flint; in other words, each blended with its setting. Just short of the summit, a track led to a redundant parsonage, a Norman church, and a Tudor mansion, Swyncombe House, standing in its own parkland. The hamlet of Swyncombe— thatched and tree-flanked—lay beyond the summit and therefore out of sight, so that the three buildings resembled a nucleus which had either strayed from or been forsaken by its particles. The church contained an apsidal end and traces of a Saxon doorway. The bell was slung from a gable in the wall because the building lacked a turret or a tower. The chancel roof was painted with stars. Everything within looked clean and cared-for. Peace dwelt among this trinity, alongside beauty and Englishry. I first discovered that fact nearly half a century ago.

Returning to the lane, I scanned the Oxfordshire acres below and the Berkshire skyline beyond them. Had the summit been slightly higher, I could have seen the River Thames, shining like a silver serpent. The vista recalled Bishop Fuller's fatherly benediction: 'Some shires, Joseph-like, have a better coloured cloak than others ... Yet every county hath a child's portion, as if in some sort observed gavel-kind in the distribution of His favours.' The Chilterns had indeed received favours. Their beechwoods were peerless; their chalk soil yielded abundant corn; their flint cottages looked as indigenous as mushrooms; their hilltops asked questions which the valleys answered, each lane and footpath unfolding a pleasant surprise, except where man had set a modern mark. Small wonder, I reflected, that no other British hills could claim such a nest of eminent poets. Milton lived for a time at Chalfont St Giles; Edmund Waller, at his ancestral home near Amersham; Shelley, at Great Marlow; Walter de la Mare, near Penn; John Masefield, at Hampden Row; G. K. Chesterton, at Beaconsfield (near to Robert Frost's *pied-à-terre*). Three famous novelists lived in the Hills; Disraeli at Hughenden; Charles Reade, at Ipsden; Rebecca West, at Ibstone. Edmund Rubbra, the composer, lived near Speen; Stanley Spencer, the artist, lived at Cookham; so also did Kenneth Grahame, author of *The Wind in the Willows*.

Walking slowly downhill, I saw again what I long ago discovered, that the Icknield Way between Bledlow and Ewelme crossed a region which, despite its relative nearness to London, retained tracts of unspoiled countryside, some of whose inhabitants revealed a Celtic lineage, for although many Celts fled westward from the Romans and Saxons, a few retreated into the remotest parts of the Chilterns, marrying among themselves, and—like some of their descendants until the early years of the twentieth century—seldom venturing far beyond their own village. Looking back forty years,

I remembered the swarthy butcher at Prestwood, who bore an ancient Chiltern surname, and was almost certainly descended from the Iberian Celts. Some scholars, indeed, believe that the word 'Chiltern' is related to 'Celt', and that both of those words can be traced to the Latin *celsus* or 'high'. In short, the Celts tended to dwell in high places. What labours, I thought, went to the making of our landscape since men first cultivated it; what trials and errors, what faith and artistry. With what greed had Trade set its mark on that heritage ... motorways, garages, aircraft, pylons, housing estates, bungalows, factories, skyscrapers, and all the other ugliness of an over-populated conveyor belt. Only by consulting old photographs could one assess the irreparable damage that had been done to the British countryside during the past half-century, and especially since the Second World War; all summarized by the fact that the Council for the Preservation of Rural England felt compelled to rename itself the Council for the *Protection* of Rural England. Fortunately, this part of Oxfordshire had escaped almost unscarred. Seeing it again, after long absence, I shared Richard Jefferies' conservatism: 'I do not want change,' he sighed. 'I want the same old and loved things; the same old flowers, the same trees ... let me find them morning after morning ... let me watch the same procession year by year.' In other words, Jefferies mourned the fact that he would one day die. Yet change is life's other name. Willy-nilly, therefore, the new look must be accepted, and its merits, if they exist, acknowledged. In any event, there are aspects of the past that cannot be weighed against the present, because we possess neither the data nor the computer with which to compare human happiness from generation to generation.

At the foot of Sliding Hill I turned left, following a metalled lane which overlaid the course of the Way. At Cow Common I turned right, and after a few hundred yards entered Ewelme, certainly the most beautiful village within sight of the Way, and possibly the most beautiful in the Chilterns. Despite a Victorian parson who rendered it as 'Ee-well-mee', the name of the village ought to be pronounced 'U-elm'. Domesday Book called it *Lawelme*, after the *aewi-elm* or 'spring of water'. Progress has tried hard to desecrate Ewelme. It has built new and therefore unseemly houses. It has slashed the sky with a tangle of wires. It has littered the weekend lanes with cars. It has unleashed aircraft that drone like morose midges. But it has not yet destroyed the medieval cottages and their hinterland of hills. Early in the morning, if you shut your eyes and ears against modernity, you may almost persuade yourself that Ewelme has not changed since its inhabitants stared at the first car ever to enter their village. Some of the cottages stand on the side of a hill, overlooking the roofs of their lower neighbours, which resemble stepping-stones, mossy and weathered. A lane girdles the village, but only a footpath among those cottages leads directly from top to bottom. On the top is a fifteenth-century church wherein a memorial recalls Colonel Francis Martyn, a Ewelme man, who, as commander of the local Roundheads, kept the church locked, and forbade his soldiers to enter it. As a result, the place escaped the Puritan pillage that marred many other parish churches. The beauty of the architecture and the aroma of the history are symbolized by the tomb of Alice, Duchess of Suffolk, from which the colours have not yet wholly faded. Four angels support her head; sixteen servers carry armorial shields; and on her left arm glows the Most Noble Order of the Garter. As though to emphasize the brevity of pomp and circumstance, the tomb bears an effigy of the dead woman's skeleton. Ewelme church is among those national heirlooms which inspired Edmund Blunden:

> heroic names,
> The gilded panel trumpeting past fames,
> Shields, pictures, solemn books of stars and sages,
> Kindled our pride in sense of mightier ages ...

Grooved by centuries of pious feet, a covered stairway

leads from the church to an almshouse which the duchess and her husband founded and endowed 'for the maintenance of two Chaplains and thirteen poor men'. During the sixteenth century the Suffolk estates escheated to the Crown, and the mastership of the almshouses was ultimately granted by King James I to the Regius Professor of Medicine at Oxford. Both sexes are now eligible for admission; election being made by the lord of the manor, the Earl of Macclesfield, who usually chooses veterans living either at Ewelme or at one of the three manors with which Ewelme was endowed. The almshouse may be likened to a miniature Oxford college. Its apartments are set around a covered quadrangle; its tranquillity is enshrined in the duchess's own description of the place, 'God's House'. She founded also the village school, which claims to be the oldest of its kind in Britain, and is assuredly the most beautiful, resembling a large manor house—gable-ended, stone-mullioned, tall-chimneyed —whose bricks are as rose-red as those at Hampton Court.

Many people have admired Ewelme. In it Henry VIII spent part of his honeymoon with Katherine Howard, niece to the Duke of Norfolk. The marriage, however, did not last long, for certain members of the Council reported that the lady was a wanton: 'Mistress Katherine Howard ... before she was joined with the king's majesty, had liv'd most corruptly ...' After an unfair trial, the Queen was attainted and executed. Henry's male heir, Edward VI, conveyed the manor of Ewelme to his sister, the future Queen Elizabeth, who spent some time there (a path is still called Queen's Walk). Prince Rupert lived awhile at Ewelme; and Jerome K. Jerome chose to be buried in the churchyard, a fitting landfall for the author of *Three Men in a Boat*, that classic of the Chilterns and the Thames.

The village watercress beds thrive (by courtesy of the *aewielm*), but the teashop-cum-general stores died decades ago. I once took afternoon tea in that shop, sitting *à deux* at the smaller of two tables, and paying the equivalent of three pence for three cakes. No charge was made for the savoury background of moth balls, cheese, sherbet, paraffin, bacon, peppermint, floor polish, linseed oil, and carbolic soap. In windy weather, whenever a customer came or went, the draught from the door provided music by tinkling an array of kettles and saucepans which hung on a string above the counter. Today that leisurely tempo has vanished. When the village inn closes, the car doors slam, the engine revs up and Time hurries home.

Although Ewelme lies within sight of the Way, it does not bestride it. I therefore returned to the foot of Sliding Hill, and stood on the Way's last green yard, once again gazing at Wittenham Clumps, at Swyncombe Downs, and at the Way itself, heading westward as a metalled lane. Where did its journey end? No one knew, though many had guessed. An eighteenth-century Bishop of Cloyne suggested that it went to Avebury, having sent an offshoot 'to Newbury, and thence it may be to Old Sarum'. Michael Drayton—never a man to be daunted by distance—suggested that the Way led to Land's End. Edward Thomas, you remember, suggested whimsically that the Way led to 'the banks of the Towy or beside the tomb of Giraldus at St David's'. Only one thing was certain; the Way went westward, across the Thames and over the Downs, into the heart of conjecture.

Finally, I glanced along the sector I had walked, which was solitary yet never melancholy; quiet until a race-track disturbed it; changed almost beyond recognition since the Celts first travelled there; during my childhood a highway for drovers and a short cut for cottagers; but now so neglected that no one followed it, except a few farmhands, and one old man with his dog, and the likes of myself. Yet how deeply the green road delved into the past, from Atomic motor-ways and Tudor mansions to medieval churches and prehistoric tumuli. Astronomers, of course, regard such a time-scale as no more than a single leaf from a brief calendar. Nevertheless, man's three-score-years-and-ten compel him to look with awe on a road that has served humanity for several millennia.

Stane Street

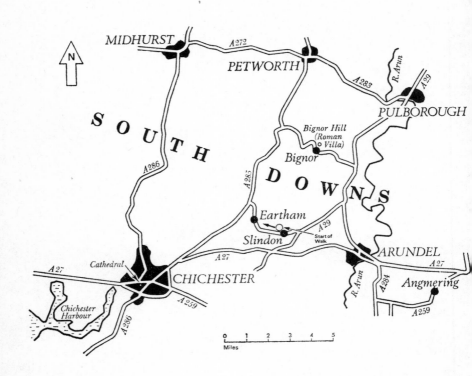

3 Stane Street

IN the year 55 BC a pedlar on the Icknield Way may have brought news of a Roman invasion. If the Celts did feel alarm, their fears subsided when, after several months, the invaders failed to appear. It is unlikely that the Chiltern folk ever learned the truth of the matter, namely, that a Roman general, Gaius Julius, had indeed landed, but that he stayed close to his ships, and sailed away after two weeks, taking with him a few hostages.

Next year the rumours of invasion were more disturbing, for the same general had landed again, but this time he marched inland to Hertfordshire, where he captured a Celtic chief, Cassivellanus, and imposed fines on the local tribes. Once again, however, no Romans reached the Icknield Way. Their leader—soon to become Julius Caesar—decided that to conquer Britain would require years of guerrilla warfare. Had he lived longer, he might have agreed that the prize was worth the price; but his rivals murdered him, and Britain remained outside the Empire, though not beyond the civilizing influence of Roman merchants, who bought British tin, corn, fleece, hunting dogs, jewellery, and ornaments.

A century later, in AD 43, the Emperor Claudius conquered the island which the Emperor Julius had invaded. From their base at Dover the Legions' first need was for roads; not green roads wandering through a land without cities, but paved roads linking the cities which Rome would build. The first major Roman road in Britain ran from Dover (*Dubrae*) to London (*Londinium*) and thence to Wroxeter (*Uriconium*), a military post on the Welsh border. The road itself came to be known as Watling Street because it traversed the territory of the *Waeclingas*, a Hertfordshire tribe.

Dover alone, however, could not supply all the requirements of the Romans, who therefore built a road from Portsmouth to London via Winchester and Staines, a devious journey, avoiding the Wealden clay. This road was augmented by another, which linked London with the small ports that were known collectively as Chichester Harbours. Instead of avoiding the Wealden clay, the second route drove through it, and became the straightest road in Britain. Every Romano-British road was partly a military route, but those that were built late, when towns had arisen, served primarily as highways for commerce and administration. Stane Street, on the other hand, was built relatively early, and therefore remained primarily a route for soldiers and local traffic.

I approached the Street from Slindon, a pleasant village six miles north-east of Chichester, the last home of Stephen Langton, whom Innocent III consecrated as Archbishop of Canterbury in 1207. Seven years later, at St Paul's Cathedral, Langton rebuked the King's misrule, thereby inspiring certain of the nobility to draw up Magna Carta. The courageous archbishop died at Slindon Manor in 1228, and now lies in the Warriors' Chapel of his own cathedral. Langton's home has disappeared; not so Eartham Hall, just beyond Slindon, formerly the home of William Huskisson, President of the Board of Trade, the first Briton to die in a railway accident. In 1830, while Huskisson was attending the opening of the line between Liverpool and Manchester, the door of a carriage threw him on to the rails at the very moment when the Rocket was approaching. Huskisson had bought Eartham Hall from William Hayley, of whom Southey remarked: 'There is nothing bad about the man except his poetry.' Hayley, in fact, was among those numerous writers whose love of literature excelled their literary achievements. He is remembered, if at all, for his friendship with William Cowper, a psychotic poet, to whom even a short journey seemed terrifying. It so happened, however, that Cowper's dearest companion, Mary Unwin, had lately suffered a stroke, and Hayley suggested that a change of air might mend the patient. Only for Mary's sake would Cowper endure the terrors of a journey from Buckinghamshire to Sussex:

> Thy silver locks, once auburn bright,
> Are still more lovely in my sight
> Than golden beams of glorious light,
> My Mary!

So, in the end, the ageing poet and his faithful companion went to Eartham. While crossing the Sussex Downs at night, Cowper experienced panic, but he arrived safely, and spent several months at the Hall, translating some of Milton's poems (and meekly accepting literary criticism from his host's twelve-year-old son).

Hayley's cultivation of a famous man did not spring solely from his own lack of fame. On the contrary, he was a genuine friend, worthy to be remembered for his perseverance in rescuing Cowper from the poverty to which the English habitually consign their poets. In 1793, hearing of Cowper's financial straits, Hayley visited the premier, William Pitt, to solicit a pension for his friend. Pitt did nothing. Hayley then visited the Home Secretary, Lord Spencer, who granted a pension of £6 weekly, which allowed Cowper to pass his remaining years in modest comfort.

Another mile or so brought me to a point where the lane crossed Stane Street, a green road running from south-west to north-east. I chose to follow the northern sector. Now the Romans believed that certain places are haunted by gods or spirits; the spirit of the woods, the spirit of the streams, the spirit of the hills. They feared those spirits. They invoked and placated them. To many people nowadays the cult seems absurd. Nevertheless, certain places continue to influence certain temperaments. A Christian visiting Bethlehem, for instance, may feel that the place is haunted by Jesus; a traveller visiting Stane Street may feel that the place is haunted by the men who made it, fifty-seven miles from Chichester to London, through some of the densest woodland in Britain. What manner of men were those Romans? And what the method of their road-making? Roman roads were made by Roman soldiers. The method varied slightly, according to the importance of the road and the nature of its subsoil, but the general procedure was as follows: on a sandy or earthen foundation the soldiers laid stones, then gravel, then more stones, then sand or earth, and finally a pavement. Each road ran on a raised causeway, from which the water was drained into marginal ditches. Extensive swamps and steep gradients were usually bypassed because the Romans did not pursue a policy of straightness at any price. The world had never before seen roads that were comparable with the Romans'; nor did such roads reappear in Britain until the eighteenth century.

Meanwhile, I took the first step forward, following the Street through Eartham Wood. It was a wide and grassy track, lit by pale February sunlight which penetrated the depths of a conifer plantation on the left. Only a robin ruffled the silence, as though to emphasize how loud the Street had been while troops felled trees, dug foundations, shovelled stones, drank wine, played dice, and stood to arms whenever a horseman galloped up with news that a band of natives were on the war-path. If the Britons had united they would certainly have repelled the Julian invasions, and might have delayed the Claudian conquest. Instead, they squandered their strength in civil war. As Edward Gibbon observed: 'The various tribes of Britain possessed valour without conduct, and the love of freedom without the spirit of union. They took up arms with savage fierceness; they laid them down, or turned them against each other with wild inconstancy; and while they fought singly, they were successively subdued.' Those suicidal seeds still germinate on British soil.

After less than a mile the trees on the left gave way, revealing open downland. On the right, too, the downs stretched to the horizon. Celia Fiennes was not exaggerating when she said that this part of Sussex contained 'up and

downe steepe hills'. Tier after tier of them arose, climbing
above Arundel. To Cumbrians and Welshmen, of course, the
Sussex Downs are mere hillocks, nowhere exceeding 870
feet above the sea; yet to the Augustans they appeared majestic. Cowper, you recall, was seized with panic when he saw
them: 'daunted', he confessed, 'by the tremendous height
of the Sussex hills'. The Downs do not maintain a continuous line, but have been eroded by several rivers, notably
the Cuckmere at Alfriston and the Arun at Arundel. Gilbert
White, sometime Vice-Provost of Oriel College, Oxford,
defined the Downs with scholarly precision: 'The range
which runs from Chichester eastward as far as East-Bourn
... is called the South Downs, properly speaking, only
around Lewes.' My previous walk along this sector had
been from north to south, so that I was now viewing the
land from a different angle; an unoccupied land, or so it
appeared, for I could see no houses, no barn, no spire, no
road; only fields and woods unfolding to the foot of distant
hills. As along Icknield Way, the map teemed with hills:
Camp Hill, Rackham Hill, Kitthurst Hill, Harrow Hill,
Highden Hill, Rewell Hill, Blackpath Hill; and the hills
either looked down on a wood or else carried it on their crest:
North Wood, Kints Wood, Findon Wood, Church Wood;
and hidden among the woods were stately homes: Muntham
Court, Angmering Park, Arundel Castle; and beyond them
lay the sea. During the early Middle Ages the Sussex Weald
was one vast woodland. But by the end of the sixteenth century the ironmasters had felled much of its timber. Smelting,
however, continued. When Celia Fiennes reached Pens-
hurst in 1697 she wrote a brief and part-punctuated account
of the business: 'there is 4 or 5 mile off a place they cast
Gunns there being a great store of oare all over the Country,
its a great charge and continuall attendance; when they have
lighted the fire for to cast bells or gunns they must be
cautiously blowing and the mettle will be apt to fall down on
the nose of the bellows and harden that if it be not still off
would quickly damm up the fire and put it out ...'

Presently the gradient stiffened while the road contracted into a footpath which soon became a narrow avenue among hazels and alders interspersed with ash, where I noticed a young tree growing in the bole of an old one. Ahead and astern the Street lay like the green shadow of a proverbial arrow. Nor was that wholly an illusion. Leaving Chichester by the east gate, at an angle of 37¼ degrees north of east, the Street held its course, without a single deviation, as far as Gumber Corner, a distance of eight miles and three furlongs. An absolutely direct route to London would need to cross several steep hills and several stretches of water; by making a few detours the Romans avoided these obstacles. Beyond Gumber the course did deviate, but soon recovered and held straight for fifteen miles, from Pulborough to Rowhook, most of which is now a metalled road. For another fifteen miles the course was so direct that no part of it veered more than two hundred yards from a straight line. After Leatherhead Down it made for Morden, Tooting, Clapham, and the site of Old London Bridge. It is still possible to trace much of the Street's course from London to Chichester, starting at Borough High Street, then crossing Watling Street near the Elephant and Castle, then proceeding down Kennington Park Road to Clapham Rise, Morden, North Cheam, Ewell, Epsom. A hiatus follows until Leatherhead Down, whereafter the course can be traced via Birchgrove, Mickleham Down, and Juniper Hall (where the old Street was called Pebble Lane, a reference to its paving). Dorking churchyard may well straddle the next sector en route for Minnickwood, Ockley, and the Pulborough road. How, then, did the Romans steer so straight? Over relatively short distances they aligned poles, rather as infantrymen 'dress by the right'. Over longer distances, or when high ground supervened, they aligned braziers. Their surveyors sometimes used a *groma* or crude direction-finder, but relied chiefly on poles and smoke. Some writers have suggested that on Stane Street the chief surveyor was a Roman engineer, Belinus, and that having driven the Street through dense woodland near Billingshurst, he gave his name to the area. It is true that in 1203 the town was called *Bellingsherst*, but in 1249 it became *Billingeshurst*, which is generally accepted as meaning the *hyrst* or 'wooded hill' of a chief called Billing.

Stane Street at this point stood several feet above the general level of the land, and from that eminence I sighted Gumber Farm, a solitary place, dear to Hilaire Belloc, author of *The Stane Street*, whose 314 pages are modestly subtitled *A Monogram*. The book appeared in 1913, almost simultaneously with Thomas's *The Icknield Way*. Its illustrations will open the eyes of those who never saw and can now scarcely imagine rural England as it was before the twentieth-century English conquered it. One picture, for example, shows a croziered shepherd on Halnacker Down, alone against a houseless horizon. Belloc himself lived long enough to witness the conversion of cornfields into car parks:

> Ha'nacker's down and England's done . . .
> And never a ploughman under the Sun,
> Never a ploughman. Never a one.

As befitted a scholar of Balliol, Hilaire Belloc was meticulous in the field work of historical studies. He walked the sites of battles, he measured the width of rivers, he sailed the curves of coasts; but he never strode the length of Stane Street, nor even a considerable tract. He preferred to explore it from a car, accompanied by Harold Baker (sometime Warden of Winchester College) and Auberon Herbert (Baron Lucas and Dingwall). Their journey was made to the tune of cold chicken and iced champagne. Belloc, in short, felt little concern for the modern Stane Street. His interests lay with military motives and topographical problems: 'the linking up of Sussex with the north', he wrote, 'was only effected by the Romans at the cost of great labour through the artificial causeway of the Stane Street between Chichester and London . . .' Belloc was no stranger to the district. His father, a Frenchman, died while the son was still a child. The widow—having lost much of her fortune through a stock-broker's incompetence—moved from France to Sussex, where her son learned to love the county, feeling an especial fondness for the River Arun and the countryside of Gumber. Perhaps he had stood where I was standing, when with a *sursum corda* he sang his own thanksgiving:

> Lift up your hearts in Gumber, laugh the Weald.
> And you most ancient Valley of Arun sing.
> Here am I homeward from my wandering.
> Here am I homeward, and my heart is healed.

It was indeed a scene to soothe, to strengthen, to assure. Gumber Farm stood like a small oasis in a vast oasis, every acre of which was both fruitful and beautiful. Man—who so often defiled the earth—had here tamed, cultivated, and adorned it; a process that reached its zenith during the eighteenth century, before human empathy was throttled by human ingenuity, and while the Age of Enlightenment was still mellowed by the wisdom of earlier ages. Belloc described these parts as 'a district of the Downs so made that when one sees it one knows at once that here is a jewel'. Another Sussex writer, Sheila Kaye-Smith, likewise spoke the truth when she said of her county: 'Here English history was born, and its earliest traces linger still in old buildings, old trees, old names, old stories.' That is not an overstatement. Into the south-east came Britain's first immigrants, ape-like men, shambling overland from what is now the Continent of Europe. Hither, when the English Channel arose, sailed the Celtic settlers. This was the landfall of Romans, Angles, Saxons, Jutes, Normans. Here St Augustine laid the founda-tions of 'the Church of England as by law established'. Here were spoken the dialects which created standard English. Through these parts came news of the world, drawn by magnetic London, a harbour, a market, a seat of govern-ment. And for centuries the news and the men and the merchandise followed the roads that Rome had built.

I gazed at Gumber Farm for a long time. The sun had

now passed its meridian, and would soon disappear behind
the hills. Before going, it emerged from a bank of clouds,
daubing the farmhouse with golden light, as in a Rowland
Hilder Sussex-scape of pasture and ploughland, flanked by
bare trees, each bough carved like a twig on the sky. North
and south, the Street was a green rampart above the fields,
a reminder that throughout the Middle Ages 'highway'
was often written as 'high way' or a road raised above the
adjacent ground. But how ill-made those roads were, more
often neglected than maintained by the parishes they traversed. Henry VIII exhorted Sussex landowners to build new
roads at their own cost, 'for the common weal of the King's
people', adding that the builders could reimburse themselves by enclosing the routes of the old roads. A century
later, Samuel Pepys felt so thankful to see roadmenders at
work he tipped them ('to menders of the highway, 6d'). A
century after that, the townsfolk of Horsham could not reach
London except by doubling back via Canterbury, a detour
which Arthur Young described as 'one of the most extra-
ordinary circumstances that the history of non-communica-
tion in this country can furnish'. Telford and Metcalf did
build paved roads, but the surfaces were less durable than
those of the Romans. In 1815 John Loudon Macadam
built the so-called 'macadamized' roads, copying methods
which had long been used in Sweden and Switzerland. Macadam insisted that no stones should be laid down if they were
too large for a roadman to place in his mouth. As a result,
much time was spent trying to swallow the building materials.
Macadam one day lost his temper when he examined a
stretch of road whose stones were far too big for any man's
mouth. Having identified the culprit, he discovered that the
roadmender was toothless.

By way of experiment I thrust my stick through the turf,
hoping to strike a Roman pavement, but Time had covered all
traces, even as it had covered the Romans. Gone was the
cursus publicus, the Imperial Mail, which carried government despatches throughout the Empire by means of couriers

who presented their *diploma* or identity card whenever they stopped to change horses or to take a bath at an official posting station. During the first century AD a message travelled from London to York more swiftly than during the seventeenth century.

Beyond Gumber Farm the Street began to climb the edge of Burton Down, a mixture of woodland and scrub, from which a clear day reveals Chichester Cathedral, a prospect that pleased Defoe when he reached Arundel: 'From hence to the city of Chichester,' he declared, 'are twelve miles, and the most pleasant and beautiful country in England, whether we go by hill, that is, the Downs, or by the plain.' As Gumber receded, the Street ceased to resemble a rampart. Erosion and tillage had obliterated all save a few traces of the raised course. By delving among some undergrowth, however, I found the embankment, several feet high and relatively wide. The entire course presented a Janus-face. Astern, it dipped like a narrow parapet; ahead, it climbed like a wide lawn; and each aspect recalled the vast period—nearly fourteen centuries—during which Britain lacked any highway that would have satisfied the Romans. Travelling through Lancashire in 1777, Arthur Young issued a warning to the nation: 'I know not, in the whole range of language, terms sufficiently expressive to describe this infernal road.' That our roads decayed when the Romans left Britain is understandable; that they remained 'infernal' for more than a thousand years thereafter is a source of wonder. Byron was not speaking too wildly when he predicted:

> While stands the Coliseum, Rome shall stand;
> When falls the Coliseum, Rome shall fall;
> And when Rome falls—the World.

Although the Greeks, too, were master-builders, their artistic bias differed from *Romanitas*, the Roman temperament. They could indeed build temples and theatres, but they could not build a Stane Street nor a Hadrian's Wall. Still less could they achieve and sustain the disciplined Roman fortitude which for centuries governed most of Western civilization. The supreme Greek attainments lay in thought and art, in Plato's *Dialogues* and in the plays of Sophocles and Aeschylus.

At the foot of Bignor Hill the Street almost lost itself on an expanse of grass. How the Romans must have cursed that hill, too steep for their liking, but not steep enough to justify a diversion. Once more I glanced back, trying to imagine the empty green road as a busy paved highway, filled with wagons hauled by oxen; with *cisia* or light carriages hauled by two fast horses (a privilege of senior officers and important bureaucrats); with peasants giving way to infantrymen who in turn gave way to cavalrymen; stray dogs, wild cats, fierce boars; flocks of sheep, herds of cattle, droves of geese; old harlots and young wives, Christian converts and pagan tipplers; humanity at large, wearing strange clothes, speaking strange words, yet at heart the same as their descendants who now fly to the moon. Even the traffic problems were not wholly dissimilar from our own, because the *cisia* often drove so recklessly that a law was passed to limit their speed. When Gaius Julius became Emperor he banned all wheeled traffic from Rome during the day.

My next lap was a steep ascent of Bignor Hill, where the Street grew narrow while climbing between trees and hedgerows. Then several other tracks appeared, making it difficult to identify the original course. But I was not the only traveller to feel puzzled. On the contrary, archaeologists still debate the matter, though all agree that on the summit of Bignor Hill the Street was a double track, divided by a high and wide bank, in all about ninety-three feet broad. Some affirm that the bank was a later earthwork; others deny it. Myself, I consulted the map, flattening it against a weather-worn oak, a symbol of the Druids who were powerful when Rome first reached Sussex. The Druids worshipped in the open air, preferably among oak groves, where they sacrificed living people to the gods. Caesar's *Commentaries* defined the Druids as a caste of privileged priests, exempt from taxation and military service: 'Attracted by these great concessions,' Caesar added, 'many young men voluntarily forgather to receive their doctrine and many are sent by parents and relatives.' Lucan, a late Latin writer, summarized the doctrine: 'The same spirit has a body again elsewhere, and death is simply the midpoint of a long life.' The Druids did not commit their creed to writing, but handed it down *viva voce* among the priests, who, according to Caesar, 'learn a great many verses by heart, and accordingly many remain as students for twenty years'. Although the Druids were exterminated by the Romans, Sussex was the last English county to embrace Christianity. The new religion reached Stane Street in the person of St Wilfred, whose sixth-century biographer, Stephanus, gave a graphic account of the saint's reception when he was wrecked on the Sussex coast. The Saxon high priest 'took his stand among his fellow-pagans, on a high mound when he cursed the people of God, and tried to paralyse them with magical incantations'. Wilfred wisely withdrew. Within a few years, however, he returned, this time more auspiciously. Having converted a local chief, he received grants of land at Pagham and Selsey, the latter becoming a bishopric which the Normans translated to Chichester.

Just short of the summit of Bignor Hill I sat down to eat my sandwiches, shielded by a belt of trees. The red sun seemed to balance itself on the brow of a distant summit while a breeze carried the tang of furrows and byres, a tang, I reflected, which to most Britons had become unfamiliar, and was unlikely ever to form part of their daily diet. It was reasonable to mourn the passing of an active and open air life, but it was not reasonable to suppose that such a life could be led by the majority of people on an overpopulated island living chiefly by manufacturing and selling factory-made wares. The Industrial Revolution would remain irreversible unless by an unimaginable upheaval. This corner of the kingdom was still quiet. Despite a relatively high population in the region, I had not met anyone during the past two hours of walking and halting. The solitude, however, meant that I had missed the old Sussex dialect, or such of it as survived. Like poetry, a patois cannot be fully translated or carried over; somewhere in mid-stream it founders and is lost. A Sussex version of *The Song of Songs* was compiled by Mark Lower, for the enlightenment of Prince Lucien Bonaparte, an amateur philologist, whom we shall encounter again in Cornwall. In that version the singer praises his lady's teeth, likening them to a flock of new-shorn sheep, and not a gap anywhere: 'Yer teeth be lik a flock of ship just shared, dat come up from de ship-wash; every one of em bears tweens, an nare a one among em is barren.' Some of the old people still use some of the old words. At Battle in 1975 I heard a roadman confess himself 'queered' or puzzled by the political situation. Near Hailsham a trug-maker informed me that he was 'properly' or extremely pleased with the corn harvest. Several of the old words were imported by Huguenot weavers: 'valiant', for example, connoting size or excellence (rather like the north country 'champion'), and 'cater' or quarter from the French *quartier*. Transport and television have not yet reduced every English dialect to the lowest level of London–Yankeedoodle.

My dog—whose dialect showed no sign of change—chose that moment to sniff a mole-hill. While scouring the turf, he raised a volley of small flints, the tools and weapons of men who lived hereabouts a hundred thousand years before the Romans built Stane Street. Known as Sussex Man, those primitive creatures died with the final Ice Age. There is indeed a limit to the power of human imagination, for although I accepted, I could not wholly assimilate, the fact that elephants once roamed where I sat. Reality did become a shade less unreal when I remembered that Sussex Man had grappled with the poignancy of death, and that when he buried his kin, he interred also a morsel of meat and a handful of flints to sustain them in the next world.

Bignor Hill is a grassy plateau, speckled with bushes and trees, forming part of three thousand acres that were given to the National Trust by F. J. W. Isaacson in 1950. One of several signposts on the summit points Latinly to *Londinium*. In summertime the plateau is covered with cars, but on a February afternoon it is very much as I found it, empty and at peace. There the green road became a metalled lane descending through woods in which it is possible to find traces of Stane Street that have survived ploughing and planting.

After about a mile the lane emerged from the trees. Then it zig-zagged through a wide valley, passing on the left a farmhouse with flower-filled gardens on each side of the lane. Just beyond the house the lane formed a T-junction with a lane leading to Bignor; and from that junction a short track led to the site of a Roman villa, now preserved as an ancient monument. Set on rising ground, the villa faced the slopes of Bignor Hill, which loomed like a green cliff on a red sky. Belloc rated the scene as 'one of the most solemnly beautiful sites of South England, covering a general slope that looks right at the dark walls of the Downs'. Bignor Villa was built during the first, and then rebuilt during the second, centuries AD. During the fourth century it began to decay, probably about the year 367, when Picts and Scots joined with Saxons to invade a large area of Southern Britain. Discovered by a farmer in 1811, the site was soon afterwards excavated by Samuel Lyons, to whom we owe the remnants of one of the biggest houses in Roman Britain, said by some to have been the residence of the Governor of the Province of Regum.

Every Roman regarded his home as a shrine; that is, a place haunted by gods whom he must please and, if necessary, placate. The poet Horace assumed that human happiness must include a home and a good wife: *Domus et placens uxor*. Throughout most of the Empire the well-to-do Romans designed their houses on the Italian model, setting it around a courtyard in order to obtain the maximum of shade. In Britain, where they needed to obtain the maximum of sunlight, they designed their houses as a series of rooms leading to an inner corridor whose ends turned back through a right-angle, like the letter E without its central extension. The typical Roman house had only one storey. The roof was tiled, and the floors were paved with vivid mosaics (those at Bignor show Venus, Winter, Ganymede, and other symbolic figures). Rich families favoured the sort of pottery that is commonly called Samian, though it originated at Arezzo in Tuscany. British pottery also was prized. The best of it came from Castor-on-Nene (*Castor Dubrioviae*) whence it was exported via Ermine Street. The Samian ware at Bignor may have been made at Pulborough, about six miles northward along Stane Street, where moulds were found. Bignor's inner courtyard was two hundred feet long and one hundred and fourteen feet wide, flanked by four corridors, three of them leading to living quarters. The eastern side contained cold, tepid, and hot baths. Some of the living rooms were centrally heated, and the sanitation was better than in many British homes today. Bignor Villa may be likened to the Georgian residences which the British built in New England, models of elegant luxury never before seen by the aborigines. The analogy, however, must not be pressed too far, because the Roman concept of *imperium* differed from the British. At no time did Rome bestow self-government on her subject peoples. Britain, by contrast, not only prepared her colonies for self-government but also gave it to some that were manifestly unready to receive it. As long ago as 1784 the first Governor-General of Bengal, Warren Hastings, paid tribute to the Babel of castes and creeds and races whom he ruled: 'Every instance which brings their real characters home to natural observation,' he maintained, 'will impress us with a more vigorous feeling for their natural rights.' Nor was that all. Hastings foresaw that the sun would, and ought, to set on the British Empire, but not (he hoped) until *imperium* had done what it could to improve the cultural and material heritage of the various dominions. Indian religion, he predicted, 'will survive when the British dominion in India shall long have ceased to exist'. No Roman governor could have written like that because no Roman governor could have felt like that. Two things, said Cicero, never will be yielded by Rome: Empire and Liberty (*imperium et libertas*).

Stane Street was out of sight when I left Bignor, yet the Roman legacy remained, both visible and audible. I saw it in the parish church, for had not the Emperor Constantine chosen Christianity as the imperial creed? I heard it when a villager used the word 'pedestrian' (Latin *pedes* or 'feet'). I heard it again when another villager inquired about the time of the bus (Latin *omnibus* or 'available to all'). Modern Britain is rooted in Roman Britain. For nearly five hundred years Rome deterred the British from tribal war and family feud. She showed them that it was possible to build splendid roads, comfortable houses, stately offices. She imposed the rule of law on the misrule of disorder. She fostered whatever was good in contemporary culture, while suppressing much that was bad. Though her radiance may now seem dim, she was in her day the light of the Western world. Scant thanks she received, and not a surfeit of profit; and when at last she quit this island, the British were conquered by barbarians more virile than themselves. Nevertheless, Rome's legacy abides. Our roads follow it; our religion is based on it; our law was touched by it; our literature is steeped in it. Even fifty years ago the majority of educated Britons possessed some Latin, which they used as a key wherewith to unlock the deep thoughts and high eloquence of antiquity. '*Roma aeterna*,' boasted Tibullus: 'Rome is immortal.' If by 'immortal' he meant 'deathless', then Tibullus was mistaken; but if he meant that Rome would exert a perdurable influence, then he was so far justified that, nearly two thousand years later, Hilaire Belloc admitted: 'The foundation of England is a Roman foundation.'

The sun was setting when I left, suffusing the sky as though an enormous bonfire blazed from the west. The glow touched Bignor Hill and on it Stane Street, which now looked lonelier than ever. 'Ichabod,' it seemed to say, 'the glory has departed.' When I first began to study Roman history I was deeply moved by the physical danger and mental anguish of those Romans who lived at a time when their Empire declined and fell, dragging with it not only the arts and graces of life but also the last vestige of Roman integrity, leaving western civilization to be plundered by tribesmen. It did not then cross my mind—indeed, it would have appeared inconceivable—that I was to witness the decline and fall of the British Empire, and the descent of millions of strangers on to this small and overpopulated island. Least of all did I think it possible that an Englishman would one day be reviled for lamenting the slow dilution of his fellow-countrymen.

Offa's Dyke

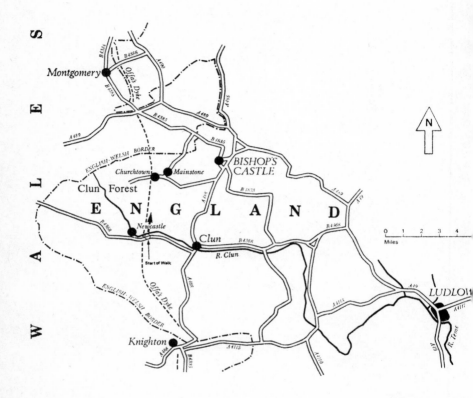

4 Offa's Dyke

WHILE Stane Street was being built, many Britons shouted 'Romans, go home!' Before the grass had begun to cover Stane Street, many Britons were shouting 'Romans, come back!' But the Romans had gone for ever, vainly trying to repel the barbarians from Rome itself. Deserted by the Legions that had defended them, the Britons, too, were invaded. Bede described their plight: 'They sent messengers to Rome with piteous appeals for help, promising perpetual submission if only the Romans would drive out the invaders.' Bede then quoted a part of that appeal: 'The barbarians drive us into the sea, and the sea drives us back to the barbarians.' The prosperous Roman province became a no-man's-land of tribes that fought among themselves even while they were being invaded by Germanic and Scandinavian pirates. Grass grew on the roads and then among the rubble of ruined cities. All the riches and culture which Rome had nurtured burst like a bubble. Five centuries later, King Alfred complained that few of his literate subjects could translate a simple Latin text.

During the eighth century, however, the islanders began to fuse their elements into a hybrid whole which we call the English nation. Although political disunity continued, it was mitigated south of the Humber by the primacy of a *Bretwalda* or British Overlord, who granted land to lesser lords in exchange for military and monetary aid. During the second half of the century the *Bretwalda* was Offa, King of Mercia, a realm stretching from the Shires to the Marches, and from Lancashire to Oxfordshire. Having styled himself *Rex Anglorum* (King of the English), Offa reasserted his primacy by styling himself *Rex totius Anglorum* (King of all the English), a distinction similar to that which would one day set the Archbishop of Canterbury above the Archbishop of York. Offa was certainly a powerful leader. He dealt as an equal with Charlemagne; he founded Saint Alban's Abbey; he minted coins, some of which circulated as far afield as Baghdad; and he built a dyke or earthen rampart from the River Dee in Wales to the River Wye in England. Some historians believed that the dyke served solely as a defence against the Welsh; others, that it served solely as a boundary mark; others, again, that it served as both. The third hypothesis seems the most convincing. Offa, surely, would not have marked such a long frontier with such a costly monument; nor could he have permanently defended the whole of it. Hadrian's Wall, for example, was shorter than Offa's Dyke, yet nearly twenty thousand men were needed to patrol and maintain it. The dyke probably served as a highway for troops moving to any point where an attack had occurred or seemed imminent.

I chose to explore a sector of the dyke in Shropshire, only a few miles from the little town of Clun, one of a famous quatrain :

> Clunton and Clunbury,
> Clungunford and Clun,
> Are the quietest places under the sun.

Housman's tribute to tranquillity was written before millions of Britons had destroyed tranquillity by visiting it. At holiday time, therefore, Clun is quiet no longer. But I arrived ahead of holiday time, early on a May morning, and found venerable houses on a hill overlooking a medieval bridge across the River Clun, where the ruined keep of a Norman castle rises dramatically from a knoll above the water. Clun Castle was built by the de Says, who gave their name to Stokesay and Hopesay. Passing by marriage to the Fitzalans, the castle was acquired by, and still belongs to, the Dukes of Norfolk. This fortress so impressed Sir Walter Scott that he portrayed it as the Castle of Garde Doloreuse

in *The Betrothed*. Clun contains a miniature square and
also an almshouse, the Holy Trinity Hospital, founded by
the Earl of Northampton in 1610. The almsfolk no longer
wear their colourful livery, nor do they dine together in hall;
but the lawns and quadrangle are almost as intimate as
those of the almshouse at Ewelme beside the Icknield Way.

North-west of Clun, not far short of Newcastle, I reached
Offa's Dyke, which at that point crossed the road. Turning to
a signpost, I entered a field, only to find that the dyke was
an inconspicuous mound, eroded by a thousand years of
tillage and climate. In the middle of the first field I halted
to con the landscape. Behind me and ahead stood a ridge of
high ground. To left and right the valley wormed its way
among hills. In the middle of the second field I halted
again, this time to con the weather, or, more precisely to
admire it. As along the Icknield Way, the sun beamed on my
journey, answering a famous question:

> What is so sweet and dear
> As a prosperous morn in May ...

At the far end of the next field, beside a stream, I reached
a black-and-white farmhouse, vivid as a mushroom in a
meadow. Parts of the house were crazily asymmetrical, rather
like the medieval houses at Lavenham in Suffolk. Earlier
generations had been obliged to ford the stream, but I crossed
via a small bridge. This was Mary Webb's domain: 'A
country,' she called it, 'where the dignity and beauty of ancient things lingers long.' Shropshire's name is often short-
ened to 'Salop', an abbreviation of *Salopescire*, the Normans'
name for the Saxons' *Scrobbesbyrigscir*, the county whose
capital is Shrewsbury or *Scrobb's burg*; Scrobb himself being the father of the Richard who, *c* 1050, built Richard's
Castle, just across the Herefordshire border. If, like many
another Norman lord, Scrobb was brusque, then etymo-
logists are justified when they suggest that his was a nick-
name, *skrobb* or gruff fellow.

Some of the surrounding hills exceeded a thousand feet,

yet the dyke scaled them undaunted. Not even the Romans would have built such a switchback. Admittedly, the course kinked a good deal while avoiding the summit of Graig Hill, but the map showed how swiftly it recovered, running with near-Roman straightness for several miles, undeterred by contours. After perhaps two miles the green road descended and then crossed a lane through a very beautiful valley. There, by appointment, I met two friends who would accompany me on the steepest sector. Robert Louis Stevenson was all for solitude on such occasions, at any rate if the walk was to be prolonged. Such ventures, he insisted, 'should be gone upon alone, because freedom is of the essence; because you should be able to stop and go, and follow this way or that, as the freak takes you; and because you must have your own pace, and neither trot alongside a champion walker, nor mince in time with a girl'. Solitude and fellowship have each their merits, and on this journey I leavened the one with the other by choosing a walker who did not expect me to trot, and also his wife, who, being a grandmother, did not require me to mince. We lunched in bright sunshine, talking partly of the dyke and partly of May in merriest mood, for the breeze sailed a few clouds on the sky, and the birds spoke by singing, as if the world were an opera. In short, it was the kind of day that prompted Vita Sackville-West to preach a brief sermon:

> Let us forget the sorrows: they are there
> Always, but Spring too seldom there ...

Refreshed and resolute, we went on our way, up a steep track past a solitary cottage, the home of an elderly couple who relished their seclusion. I asked them whether many other walkers came this way. 'No,' they replied, 'not many. In winter, hardly a soul.' Chiefly youngsters? 'Lord bless you, no. All ages. Last week we'd a party of old folks. They didn't walk very far, but at least they got out and climbed where you're going.' The news heartened us because the hill ahead suggested that we were going to heaven; an illusion which increased when the dyke grew tall, and the foss beside it deep. Half-scrambling to the summit, we saw the green road swooping down again, dizzier than ever. Down, then, we went, marvelling at the hawthorn blossom, white as a scented cloud. On the next summit we reached a plateau and a few hundred yards of level going wide enough to carry several tractors abreast. Not a house was visible. As along Stane Street, I pictured the men who had toiled there, felling trees, shovelling earth, piling debris from the foss onto the dyke; but whereas Stane Street was the work of Roman soldiers, Offa's Dyke was the work of Saxon peasants. The Welsh regarded all Mercians as *Saison* or Saxons, a name that was sometimes given to every non-Celtic inhabitant of Britain. Bede, for example, described the multiracial Germanic invasion as *aduentos Saxonum*, the arrival of the Saxons. Rome rated the Saxons as barbarians, though in Offa's day they were probably the least uncouth Britons, excelling the Celts both as farmers and as sailors. Although we classify ourselves as members of the Anglo-Saxon race, we possess very few tangible relics of our Saxon heritage. A Saxon church is rare indeed; a Saxon dwelling, rarer still. Nevertheless, from the Dark Ages onward, most of the English came of Germanic stock. Even today the Welsh use *Saison* as a collective description of all Englishmen. The intangible aspects of the Saxon heritage are difficult to unravel. Aelfric suggested that the Saxons struck a balance between an absolute and a limited monarchy by electing their King and thereafter accepting the rough with the smooth: 'Once anointed,' he wrote, 'the King has authority over his people, and they may not lawfully shake off their yoke.' Voltaire's *Lettres Sur Les Anglais* claimed that the Saxons were pioneer parliamentarians: 'The barbarians who came from the shores of the Baltic, and settled in the rest of Europe, brought with them the form of government called the States or Parliaments, about which so much noise is made ...' Our shires, or what remains of them, began as

Saxon divisions of land. Some of the days of our week are named after a Saxon god (Woden's Day, Thor's Day, Frig's Day). When the Saxons became Christians they excelled as copyists and illuminators of manuscripts, notably the Lindisfarne Gospels. Compared with the Romans, however, the Saxon architects were as children. *The Anglo-Saxon Chronicle* believed that the ruined Roman cities had been built by a race of supermen: 'Cities visible from afar, the cunning work of giants, the wondrous fortifications that are on this earth.' The peasants who built Offa's Dyke understood that they were living in a dark age, a derelict aftermath of civilization. 'Thus,' cried one of their poets, 'the Creator of men laid waste this kingdom, until ... the old works of the giants stood desolate.' On the English language the Saxons left a lasting imprint, not least among our place-names. Along the eastern perimeter of the dyke the Saxon imprint was accentuated by the Celtic place-names along the western perimeter. Thus, Newcastle was a Saxon version of *novum castellum* or 'new Roman fortification'; Lydbury was *Hlidiaburg*, a *burg* or 'settlement' on a *hlid* or 'slope'; Mainstone was *maegenstan* or 'large rock'.

Suddenly the dyke veered from north-west to north-east, seeking the least difficult way across a stream and over the hills. The map still showed several place-names beside the dyke, but not a single village. Continuing north-east, we reached Skeltons Bank, a tautological name, 'bank' being a Shropshire word for 'hill', and *scelftun* being a Saxon word for 'hill settlement'. The only settlement we could see was one hilltop house beside a lane that meandered from Three Gates to nowhere in particular. When the dyke crossed that lane our footsteps echoed briefly on a metalled surface, and then subsided into the turf of a green road which seemed to have been erupted by a huge mole. Wales lay only a mile or two westward from the dyke, and several Welsh place-names appeared to the east of it: Llanfair Hill, Castle Idris, Bryn-mawr, Pant-y-Lidan, Cefan Hepress, Maesgwyn, Bettws-y-crywyn. How old is that language? The Welsh claim that Late British became Primitive Welsh during the sixth century. Two hundred years later, when the earliest written texts appeared, Primitive Welsh gave way to Old Welsh, whereafter the language changed so slightly that a modern Welsh-speaker can understand the documents of his pre-Norman ancestors, whereas an Englishman must learn a strange language if he would read *Beowulf* in the original. During the sixth century the Welsh language was far more widespread than it is today, chiefly because the Celts had not then been Saxonized. It was spoken in southern Scotland and in western England, so that a British Celt travelling from Edinburgh to Cornwall via Cumberland would have found an intelligible tongue throughout his journey. The language was introduced to Brittany by Welsh and Cornish immigrants. At late as the 1890s the Breton fishermen improvised a patois that enabled them to communicate with their Cornish colleagues.

On the next hill, which was thirteen hundred feet high, I tried to sight an even loftier summit, a few miles south-west, on which stood the Shropshire church of Bettws-y-crywwyn, whose name (*bettws* or 'chapel' and *crywyn* or 'pigsty') suggested a division of labour between things spiritual and things temporal. Did William Cantlin follow the dyke en route to his death at Bettws? In so far as Cantlin was a pedlar, it is possible that he did follow the dyke; more than that we cannot say, because Cantlin's death is the only recorded fact of his life. But we do know that in 1691 he visited Bettws, probably to do business there. We know also that he collapsed and soon afterwards died. The site of his death is marked by the Cantlin Stone: 'W. C. Decsd. here. Buried 1691 Bettws.' Despite the fact that in those years a commercial traveller was classified as vagrant, the men of Bettws buried Cantlin at their cost. Nearly two centuries later, while Clun Forest was being enclosed and partly redistributed among adjacent parishes, the authorities discovered that Bettws had once given Christian burial to a poor pedlar. By way of belated reward, therefore, the parish received several hundred extra acres of forest. In Cantlin's day the forest contained a considerable number of Welshmen, who called themselves *cymry* or 'fellow-countrymen'. The name 'Wales' is a corruption of *wealas*, the Saxon for 'aliens' and a synonym for 'slaves'. It is difficult to estimate the amount of fighting that occurred on the dyke. Private feuds certainly took place, but nothing comparable with Flodden Field, where the armies of England and Scotland met in formal battle. The subjugation of Wales did not begin until William the Conqueror sent three trusted friends to govern the Welsh Marches from castles at Shrewsbury, Hereford, and Chester (the Roman *castra*, which became a royal palatinate). Each side of the Border remained subject to its own laws. Welsh affairs were handled by Welshmen; English affairs, either by an Englishman or by a Norman. Edward I increased the pressure by building several castles in the heart of Wales. Then he softened and also strengthened the blow by creating his eldest son the first Prince of Wales. Threatened by Scotland and France, no medieval King of England could have tolerated a hostile Wales. However, when the Principality was tamed, the powers of the Lords Marchers passed to the President and Council of Wales and the Welsh Marches, which sat usually at Ludlow Castle, and occasionally at Bewdley, Tewkesbury, Gloucester, and other places near the border. During the reign of Henry VIII three Statutes were passed, joining Wales with England. The second of these, 'An Act for the laws and justice to be administered in Wales in like form as in this realm,' is commonly called the Act of Union. At that time no other solution was possible. At a later time an accident of birth allowed James VI of Scotland to become James I of England, thereby confirming that Britain, like Brentford, would henceforth accommodate only one King.

When we were half-way down the next slope a breeze stirred, just brisk enough to dislodge some of the hawthorn blossom. The petals curtseyed to the ground like snowflakes miming the note-by-note descent which Bruckner evoked

from the falling chords of his Fifth Symphony. Near the foot
of the slope we passed an immense lime tree, which suggested yet another division of labour among the arts, because the tree was repeating audibly in colour an effect which
Tennyson achieved silently in black-and-white: 'the mur-
muring of innumerable bees'. The dyke was now as tall as a
man, and the gradient steeper. Approaching the umpteenth
summit, we reached Middle Knuck Farm, from which the
vista was wider than ever. Some of the hills were only two
miles away, while others stood deep in Wales, and a few
dominated the distant parts of England. Suddenly—in the
middle of the farmyard—the dyke disappeared. We could
see the rest of it, climbing high ahead; but of any path
leading to it we saw nothing at all, nor anything of the
farmer or his family. Like Clun itself, Middle Knuck Farm
was among 'the quietest places under the sun'. After much
wandering, we did find a way of escape; and on we went, still
climbing, convinced that Upper Knuck Farm—if, indeed,
it existed—must lie in the ionosphere, harvesting manna and
other celestial crops.

Like Ahab, King Offa coveted his neighbour's land. In
fact, he set the dyke as far to the west as seemed politic. But
why did he build a second dyke, known as Wat's Dyke, a few
miles to the east, running parallel with its more famous twin?
No one has yet answered that question. All we know is, that
Wat's Dyke can be traced from the River Dee near Basing-
werk to a point near Oswestry. In verse, however, the two
dykes were joined by Thomas Churchyard, son of a Shropshire farmer, who was born about 1520. After serving as a
mercenary in Scotland, Ireland, the Netherlands, and France
(where he was taken prisoner), Churchyard escaped to England, and achieved some fame as a poet and military historian. At the age of seventy he received a pension from
the Queen. Fourteen years later he died, unlamented by
Edmund Spenser who dismissed him as an ancient medio-
crity, 'Old Palaemon, who sung so long until quite hoarse
he grew.' Churchyard's contribution to the literature of the

dyke echoes the style of Drayton's *Polyolbion*, and shares
some of its dubious historiography:

> There is a famous thing
> Called Offa's Dyke, that reacheth farre in length.
> All kinds of wares the Danes might thither bring.
> It was free ground, and called the Britons' strength.
> Watt's Dyke, likewise, about the same was set,
> Between which the two the Danes and Britons met,
> And traffic still, but passing bounds by sleight,
> The one did take the other pris'ner straight.

Above Middle Knuck the going became almost too steep,
and we were thankful to reach a short level sector. The hawthorn blossom was so profuse that we agreed to refrain
from remarking on it; but nothing could silence our delight
at the beauty of the weather and the landscape. Green hills
rose up on all sides, as spacious as the Cheviots, and less bare.
Several of the peaks carried woods; many were grazed by
sheep. Far below, the vale sparkled with wheat, pastures, and
one or two farmsteads shining like white dishes on a baize
table. Just such a prospect may have prompted William
Camden to hail the English scene as 'a Master-Piece of
Nature, perform'd when she was in her best and gayest
humour'. That the scene had evolved gradually and by
accident from earthquake and erosion, and that men themselves had moulded it, did not lessen our sense of awe. On
the contrary, it recalled the testimony of eminent judges
such as Andrew Young, a Scottish poet, who rated the Shropshire highlands as 'a country so sweet and yet so impressive
that it might be considered the most beautiful part of England'. John Masefield, a native of the Marches, spent his
early childhood under the same bi-lingual spell: 'I looked
at the shadowy land like a dim cloud on the horizon, and
knew from my elders that that was Wales, the land of the
Welsh, who were not English, but a foreign race.' Another
Marcher poet, Mary Webb, saw the scene as a demi-Eden:
'The country that lies between the dimpled lands of Eng-

land and the gaunt purple steeps of Wales—half in Faery and half out of it.' Yet the fey was founded firmly on Wenlock limestone, Clee Hill Granite, Grinshill Freestone, and the Wrekin's Cambrian antiquity. From those rocks arose a necklace of Marcher castles: Bridgnorth, Hopton, Stokesay, Clun, Tong, Myddle, Shrewsbury, and others too numerous to litanize.

The further we travelled, the more we agreed that Offa's Dyke was not designed as a type of Hadrian's Wall. Even a cursory glance showed that the Mercians had trusted as much to the gradients as to their own workmanship. History, too, exposed the dyke's weakness as a barrier. In 1055, for example, the Welsh swept over it unchecked, to ravage England beyond the Severn. Likewise the Lords Marchers found it no impediment when they led punitive expeditions into Wales. Yet the dyke did act as a deterrent, especially against raiders trying to steal English livestock. William the Conqueror strengthened the deterrent by ordering that if an armed Welshman were caught on the English side he should lose his right hand.

At the end of the level sector we came face to face with a depth and a height more daunting than any that we had yet descended and climbed. The dyke was dishevelled, the English side being covered with scrub while the Welsh side slid down the edge of a wood, Cwm Frydd. Even to descend that slope was difficult; to have built it, with no more than gardening tools, was indeed a feat of stamina. Like the Roman Senators, the Saxon Kings employed slaves to do the dirtiest of their work; but whereas imperial Rome was a society of classes, Saxon England was a society of castes. St Paul, a Jew, was also a Roman citizen, entitled to appeal to Caesar: *Civis Romanus sum*. The men who built Offa's Dyke were not equal under the law. Their rights and obligations varied with caste, which comprised their groups: first came the *thanes*, of whom the greatest might be called noblemen, and the least might be called squires. Thanes were primarily warriors, landowners, and administrators. As such, they maintained a tradition which Tacitus recorded: 'It is considered a lifelong infamy and reproach to survive the chief and withdraw from battle. To defend him ... is the essence of sworn allegiance. The chiefs fight for victory, the followers fight for their chief.' Second came the churls, who might be called freeholders of a small property, though the size of their holdings varied from region to region, and some of the holdings were leased. Churls were primarily farmers and craftsmen. Third came the slaves, who were bought and sold at public auctions, a sturdy young male being valued at the price of eight oxen. In theory a Saxon slave possessed certain rights; in practice he lived and died at the whim of his master. Seldom, if ever at all, did a Saxon slave achieve the position which some Roman slaves enjoyed as their master's secretary and friend. The Church, however, strove to mitigate the hardships of Saxon slavery and to encourage manumission, the granting of freedom.

It was at this point, on the edge of Cwm Frydd, that we met our only fellow-travellers en route, a party of small boys toiling uphill, burdened by their camping equipment. Glad of an excuse to halt, the leader asked us what the time was. We told him, and in exchange learned that the travellers were Boy Scouts from Solihull near Birmingham. Their knowledge of Offa, we suspected, was minimal. Some of the youngest Scouts probably regarded him as 'the bloke wot owns it'. But their zeal for adventure outweighed their lapse from scholarship. Each of us having traversed a country which the other was about to explore, we compared notes and then went our ways; the Scouts to the level sector, ourselves into the valley, all the while watching a familiar illusion whereby every downward step seemed to raise the hills ahead. After a few hundred yards the gradient slackened, the trees and scrub receded, and we entered a narrow valley, topped by that daunting skyline. The valley itself contained a small church, two cottages, and a stream, the Unk, which we crossed by means of a plank. The only sign of life was a dog, barking from a caravan beside the water. One of the cottages was old and decaying. The other—relatively modern and evidently occupied—evoked a mood which Edward Thomas experienced when he, too, sighted a cottage in a secluded valley : 'The stranger sees a quiet house embowered in green against which its smoke rises like a prayer, and he imagines that he could be happy there as he had not until now been happy anywhere.'

The map confirmed that we were in Churchtown, a hamlet of Mainstone, a Saxon settlement on the edge of Wales, whose name may have referred to a stone near the church. A man at Clun had told me that the stone, weighing two hundredweight, was formerly used as a test of strength, the aspirant being required first to lift it and then, if he could, to throw it over his shoulder. It may appear strange that a hamlet should ever have been called a town; but town is simply *tun*, a Saxon word which, like the Greek *zaun*, meant either a hedge or an enclosure, and ultimately came to mean the house or houses within that enclosure. Thus, Dent Town in Yorkshire is a small village, and Lizard Town in Cornwall is smaller still.

Accompanied by bird song, we entered the church (rebuilt 1887), finding there a Tudor oak roof and panelling, and an altar cloth of 1673. The place was so well kept that we were puzzled to see many droppings on the floor. Had the rats run amok since the previous cleaning? Our question was answered by a framed notice which thanked the parish ladies who waged constant war against *bats*. Was it, we wondered, beyond the power of science to exterminate a few flying creatures in a small building?

The weather being perfect, and the afternoon still young, we made a short detour in search of Mainstone, following a lane beside the Unk, past the ruins of a handsome village school which, in years gone by, had taught the children all they needed to know ... the three Rs, a smattering of history and Bible tales, the local flora and fauna, and the merits of belonging to a small community of farmfolk. But times had so changed that in 1976 this kingdom, once famous for its beef and dairy produce, had almost ceased to make butter, almost ceased to make cheese, and did not breed enough beef to feed its own inhabitants. At Mainstone, meanwhile, we found only a house or two, a farm or two, and little else except green hills, red earth, deep woods, swift streams. Yet in 1814 the village contained 61 houses and 419 inhabitants.

In the midst of that solitude we heard a car, and were surprised because half a dozen miles of dyke had steeped us in a dozen centuries of silence. The motorist, too, was surprised, not so much by the sight of human beings as by the fact that they were walking. He therefore offered to carry us to our destination, on the assumption that only a fool or a felon willingly walks anywhere. The same assumption prevailed two centuries ago, to the dismay of Pastor Moritz (whom we met at Wittenham Clumps, you remember, overlooking the Icknield Way): 'A traveller on foot in this country,' he complained, 'seems to be considered a sort of wild man who is to be stared at, pitied, suspected, shunned.' When Elizabeth Bennett of *Pride and Prejudice* walked three miles for pleasure, she was rebuked for showing 'a most country-town indifference to decorum'. It is significant that the word 'pedestrian' did not appear until 1796, by which time Wordsworth was already publicizing the Lake District. Largely because of his poetry and his prose guidebook to Lakeland, walking became respectable, at any rate among literary and artistic persons. Nor was the exercise wholly an aesthetic indulgence. De Quincey, for example, confessed that he never felt really well unless he walked between eight and fifteen miles every day. Edward Thomas and Hilaire Belloc were tireless walkers. When Belloc was an Oxford undergraduate he walked from Carfax to Marble Arch in eleven and a half hours, a record that has yet to be broken. Thomas's widow said that walking was for him both a necessity and a pleasure: 'This of all his pleasures was the deepest and most comprehensive. For to Edward Thomas walking was not merely exercise. . . .' To us, also, walking was not merely exercise, so we declined the motorist's invitation to get there quickly.

Our scheduled journey ended at Churchtown, where Offa's indomitable dyke scaled a hill so steep that the mere sight of it made us feel breathless, partly at the thought of climbing it, and partly at remembrance of the men who built it, some of whom—after an accident or an affray—were buried beside their own monument. Indeed, the dyke itself resembled one of those anonymous graves that can be seen in country churchyards, a green mound without headstone or any other record. The steep hill, by the way, was called Edenhope, as if to imply that the dyke aspired hopefully towards Paradise. Poetry, however, is not the same as etymology. 'Edenhope' was a corruption either of *Ea-denu* (a valley with a river) or of *Eada's hop* (the territory of a chief named *Eada*). In any event, it would be wrong to suppose that Offa was the only dyke-builder. On the contrary, the Dark Ages raised a network of dykes from Scotland to Cornwall, each serving as a frontier and shield for local tribes. Offa himself was checked by a dyke which the West Saxons built against Mercians who raided Wessex. Since the dyke stretched for sixty miles across Somerset and Wiltshire, many of the Saxons attributed it to a god, Woden; whence the name Wansdyke.

Had life been longer, or the dyke shorter, we might have climbed Edenhope Hill en route for the green road's northern terminus. Instead, we imagined the road recrossing the Unk as a metalled lane; then bearing north-west in order to avoid Caer Din, a hilltop site, nearly 1,400 feet among the larks; then bearing north-north-west, still as a metalled lane, and for several miles following a more or less straight course to Lower Edenhope, where it once more became a green road, passing the woods at Mellington Hall; then reverting briefly to a metalled lane; then, at Brompton Hall, resuming its grassy way north-north-west until it came within sight of Montgomery Castle, and so entered Wales, at a place where it had certainly been sighted, and may have been explored, by three famous men. The first of this trio was John Donne, Dean of St Paul's, who stayed at Montgomery Castle, and wrote a poem about the hill on which it stands, *The Primrose, Being at Montgomery Castle, Upon the Hill, On Which It is Situate,*

> Where, if Heav'n could distil
> A shower of rain, each several drop might go
> To be his own primrose, and grow Manna so ...

The second celebrity, George Herbert, was born in 1593, either at the castle or in the adjacent Black Hall, both of which belonged to his grandfather. Cutting short the promise of a brilliant career as scholar and courtier, Herbert became vicar of a remote Wiltshire parish, where, besides writing poetry, he fulfilled his own definition of a good country priest: 'His parish is all his joy and thought.' The third writer, Edward Herbert—a kinsman of George—became first Baron Herbert of Cherbury, taking his title from an English village within a mile or two of Montgomery. Born in 1583, Lord Cherbury wrote an amusing *Autobiography* (not published until Horace Walpole got hold of it in 1764) and also *The Life and Reigne of King Henry the Eighth,* which contains an anglicized Welshman's approval of the union of England and Wales: 'The king, now considering that it was but reasonable to unite this part of the kingdom to the rest ... caus'd an act to be past for executing justice in Wales, in the manner as in England.' The turbulence of Tudor life near Offa's Dyke is cited in a passage from Lord Cherbury's *Autobiography*: 'My grandfather was noticed to be a great enemy to the outlaws and thieves ... who robbed in great numbers in the mountains of Montgomeryshire....'

But all that lay far behind, even as the dyke stretched far ahead. Under the lee of Edenhope Hill our own journey ended, and we made arrangements to rejoin the world as quickly as possible. Unlike myself, my companions were global travellers, yet they both agreed that the scenery and the weather and the dyke itself had created an experience which we would not soon forget. My own summing-up reached a similar verdict. In so far as it was neither a commercial highway nor a garrisoned defence, Offa's Dyke lacked the numinous aura of the Icknield Way and Hadrian's Wall; but in so far as it had been built by our ancestors, through the most beautiful region of England, Offa's Dyke was indeed a monument to human endeavour; and although its original purposes were outdated, its grassy solitude remained a haven for anyone seeking respite from the busyness of getting and spending.

The Abbot's Way

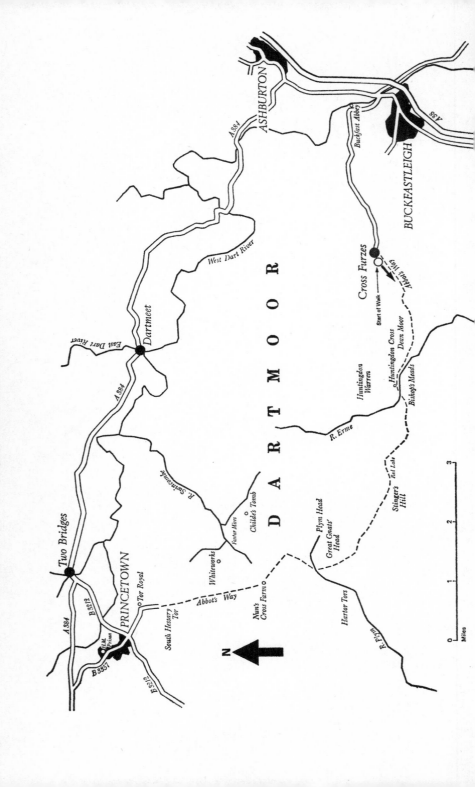

5 The Abbot's Way

OFFA'S DYKE was a product of the Dark Ages, a period when Britain's ethnic groups were still in a state of warlike disunity. The Abbot's Way was a product of the Middle Ages, a period when Celts, Jutes, Angles, Saxons, Vikings, and Normans merged as a nation, but with little awareness of what is now meant by nationalism. This may seem paradoxical because, for the first time in its history, England under the Normans was ruled by one King and by him alone. He owned every inch of the realm, both in theory and in practice. Even the greatest of the nobles were tenants who received their estates from the King, in return for fulfilling certain obligations, such as attendance at Court and service during war. Likewise the lesser nobles received estates from the greater, and were themselves bound by comparable obligations. So, the pyramid of State descended from the King to the humblest of his subjects who tilled his own strips of land, and followed his lord to the wars. The pattern of feudalism varied from region to region, but its basis was everywhere the same, being fealty to an overlord and ultimately to the King. England during the early Middle Ages was a confederation of regions that were simultaneously knit and transcended by international Christendom, which embraced the whole of Europe, and was symbolized by the Papacy. Rome, in short, had arisen phoenix-like from her own ashes. To Rome men still looked for leadership. Finding that the Emperor of Rome was no longer all-powerful, they turned to the Bishop of Rome, who became the chief bishop and finally the Pope or head of a Church which used its own spiritual power in order to curb the secular power of others. The men who made the Abbot's Way were therefore subjects of a King who acknowledged the Pope's primacy in religious matters, and sometimes submitted to his secular demands, according to the medieval doctrine of the Two Swords, whereby Church and State were supreme each in its own sphere. The spheres, however, overlapped, and human nature seldom agreed to compromise. Nevertheless, the medieval Church did much to soften the rigours of a brutal age. The great abbeys and cathedrals were not raised as monuments to an individual's wealth or prestige; rather, they enshrined the fact that almost every European was a Christian. Whenever a peasant heard the Sanctus bell he crossed himself. The priest blessed the plough, prayed for rain, gave thanks for the harvest. The Church presided over every aspect of a man's activity, his baptism, marriage, sickness, death, travel, war, work, recreation. A peasant was probably more secure under Henry I than under Offa, but he was neither better fed nor better housed. He remained poor, illiterate, servile. He accepted the social order as inevitable and unchangeable, a part of nature, like the climate. Yet his brief days were sustained by the hope of eternal bliss, and his nascent nationalism was curbed by three influences: first, the international ethos of Christendom; second, the preoccupation of Norman and Angevin monarchs with their territories across the Channel; third, the dialects which divided the English people.

Such was England at the time of the making of the Abbot's Way, a green road across Dartmoor, so named because it joined the two abbeys of Buckland and Buckfast. That the monks themselves created the entire route is unlikely, because Bronze Age folk had dwelt beside it, and the monks probably followed some of those ancient tracks, treading new ones to fill a gap. Sabine Baring-Gould, a Dartmoor 'squairson', believed that the moor contained several prehistoric tracks, notably the one leading from Moretonhampstead to Mis Tor via Postbridge. The history of the Way's eastern terminus at Buckfast Abbey can be traced to the ninth century. In 1086 Domesday Book stated: 'Bucestre is the head of an abbacy.' Thereafter the abbey declined until, about the year 1134, it was revived by monks from Savigny in France. Following the Dissolution the abbey was granted to Sir Thomas Denys, who, having sold the lead roof, allowed the rest to decay. In 1805 the ruins were bought by a businessman named Berry, who built a large house on the site, and a tall-chimneyed factory nearby. Eighty years later the property was acquired by a party of Benedictines from Ireland and Wales. Disliking Berry's house, the Benedictines decided to rebuild fragments of the ruined abbey and to incorporate them in a new church. Their abbot was Boniface Natter of Wittenberg, who owed his election to an influx of German monks. After a few years he perished in a shipwreck, and was succeeded by another German, Anscar Vonier, whose worldly wealth consisted of one golden sovereign, scarcely enough with which to build an abbey. However, somebody gave him an old cart; somebody else gave him an old horse; and a third party gave him a load of stone. In 1906 the brethren began their *opus Dei*, the creation of a vast abbey in the late Norman style. Twenty-six years later the abbey was formally opened by Cardinal Bourne. As, therefore, in the tenth century, so in the twentieth; the eastern terminus of the Abbot's Way belongs to the Roman Church.

From that terminus the Way leads northward as a lane to Cross Furzes, passing a Dartmoor National Park signpost at the start of the green sector. I arrived during March, in time to see the clouds gathering while the Way loped downhill, flanked on the left by a tall hedgerow. The middle distance showed pastures dipping to a wooded combe. Ahead loomed the moor, speckled with stunted trees. When I had walked about a quarter of a mile the sun disappeared, leaving the skyline more than ever sombre. At the bottom of the hill the Way entered a wood with a stream running through it, spanned by an ancient clapper bridge, a reminder that the medieval Church was the principal maintainer of bridges and roads (one of the Bishops of Ely granted Indulgences to all who repaired the road between Trumpington and Cambridge). The Church's concern for bridges is proved by the number of them that bear religious carvings. Several bridges were equipped with a chapel at which the people invoked St Christopher, the patron of travellers. Such chapels can be seen at Rotherham in Yorkshire, at Bradford-on-Avon in Wiltshire, and at St Ives in Huntingdonshire. Moreover, the laity were exhorted to subscribe as well as to labour. In Warwickshire, for example, a certain 'William Ashby, deceased, gave ... 20d unto ye mending of ye highway betwixt prats pit and the pinfold ... at Lapworth.'

While I was crossing the clapper bridge a rift in the clouds revealed the sun. For perhaps ten seconds the scene was transfigured. The stream changed from grey to blue; bare boughs reproduced themselves as black shadows; the dull grass shone. Without moving, all things leaped to life, just long enough for my camera to embalm them. Then the brightness went out, quick as a candle. The mist and drizzle were especially disappointing because, from my Exmoor home in North Devon, I could on a clear day see the distant Dartmoor mountains. Devon, in fact, is England's largest single county, for Lincolnshire and Yorkshire are now each divided into several administrative regions. When Yorkists claim that their county contains an acre for every word in the Bible, Devonians retort that their county contains an acre and a half for every word in Shakespeare. Geographers are content to admit that Devon contains more than 2,160 square miles, and is one of only three counties which span England from sea to sea.

Emerging from the wood, the Way grew steep and in some places so elusive that I steered by means of blobs of orange paint which the Park Warden had daubed on a wall. The fertile country fell astern while rock and peat drew nearer, displaying the latest phase in a process that began aeons ago when layers of molten granite were erupted over a wide area of the moor, to create a seedbed for tin, arsenic, copper, china clay. Erosion of the overlying rocks then penetrated the granite, to form a subsoil of growan at the base, and of clitters

or stones near the summits. Then the summits themselves
were split, both vertically and horizontally, to form towers
or tors. In Dartmoor's harsh climate the plants seldom rotted
completely, but turned to layers of peat.

With every step the scene became wilder, rockier, loftier.
Near a stile beside a dried-up brook the Way swerved sharp
right, still climbing. At Dean Moor it stood 1,200 feet above
sea level. There I found the site of some Bronze Age huts, as
proof that this uninhabited region was once populated. A
typical stone hut was circular, with an internal diameter of
about twenty feet. The earthen floors were sometimes
lowered in order to increase head room. A stone bench
against the wall served as seat by day and as a pillow at night.
The leather roof was slung across rafters. The builders of
those huts were hardier than Robert Herrick, a Caroline
vicar of Dean Prior on the edge of the moor. Plagued by rain
and snow, Herrick declared that he would rather emigrate to
the Arctic than live on the moor:

> let us make our best abode,
> Where humane foot, as yet, ne'er trod:
> Search worlds of Ice; and rather there
> Dwell, than in loathèd Devonshire.

Beyond Dean Moor the rocky solitude grew oppressive. I
neither heard nor saw any creature at all, not even a sheep's
skull. I could only enliven the loneliness by imagining a
party of monks plodding head-down against a gale. So, even
in this forsaken land, Rome's legacy lingered, for, as we have
seen, it was a Roman Emperor who laid the secular foundation of a church that still binds millions of people throughout the world. As Gibbon observed: 'Constantine ... from
the first moment of his accession declaring himself protector
of the church, at length deserved the appellation of the first
Emperor who publicly professed and established the Christian religion.' In that sense, therefore, Rome is still *urbs et
orbs*, both a city and a world, the creation of Popes who
transmuted a pagan empire into a Holy Roman Empire,

whose influence survived until the sixteenth century, be-
queathing a mystique so powerful that, when the last of the
Holy Roman Emperors abdicated in 1806, Britain refused to
recognize the dissolution of the Empire, asserting that the
abdication of an Emperor did not *ipso facto* dissolve an
Empire.

The monks who walked this Way were governed by the
heads of abbeys, the abbots (Aramaic *abba* or 'father'), some
of whom—the mitred abbots—sat with bishops and arch-
bishops in the House of Lords, rendering unto Caesar only
such things as were approved by the Pope. Rome, not
London, was their ultimate *nil obstat*. By the end of the
thirteenth century, however, many of the higher clergy were
neglecting their pastoral duties in favour of secular prefer-
ment. William Langland, a clerk in minor orders, complained
that several bishops no longer resided within their dioceses :

These lodge in London during Lent and at other times also.
Some serve the King and his silver count
In Chequer and Chancery Courts . . .
Their mass and their matins and canonical hours
Are said undevoutly . . .

Some degree of worldliness among the clergy was inevitable because very few medieval laymen could read and write
fluently. In so far as a Civil Service did exist, its senior members were chiefly clerics, masters of English, Norman-
French, and Latin (the Esperanto of scholarship and diplomacy). By the end of the fourteenth century the laxity had
tainted even the friars, the apostles of poverty. This decline
of spirituality can be traced in church architecture, from the
asceticism of Early English to the humanism of Late Italian.
After the Renaissance the building of churches passed from
plain masons to sophisticated architects. The *Opus Dei*, the
work of God, became *Opus mundi*, the work of man, well
paid by City Fathers and other *nouveaux-riches*. Nevertheless, whatever was merciful and civilized owed its example
to the best of the medieval clergy. Against Langland's rich

and cynical bishop must be set Chaucer's poor and devout parson:

> a povre Person of a town.
> Yet rich he was in holy thoght and work.

At Huntingdon Cross the Way turned due west, passing two medieval relics, Bishop's Meads and Huntingdon Warren, where rabbit-runs were visible as humps among coarse grass. Some of the Dartmoor warrens are seven centuries old, and each in its day contained a house for the warrener. The word 'warren' comes from *war*, the root of a Teutonic word, meaning 'to protect'. Warrens, in short, were breeding-grounds for rabbits, a valuable item of medieval diet, though nowadays rated as vermin. Soon after passing the Warren I closed my notebook because the entries had become repetitive: 'very wild' ... 'granite everywhere' ... 'rockier every yard' ... 'still getting more desolate'. This may have been the place that inspired a gloomy passage in Noel Barrington's *Dartmoor: A Descriptive Poem*:

> Nothing that has life
> Is visible; no solitary flock
> At will wide-ranging through the silent moor,
> Breaks the deep-felt monotony ...

Barrington deserves mention, not for his gift of poetry, which was slight, but for his love of Dartmoor, which was immense. He was born at Plymouth in 1777, son of a grocer. Having served as a clerk in Plymouth Dockyard and then with the Royal Navy, he taught at a Maidstone school, after which he opened his own academy at Devonport. His first book of poems, *Banks of Tamar*, appeared in 1820. Four years later the Royal Society of Literature offered a prize for a poem about Dartmoor, a subject which Barrington had explored thoroughly. His own poem, unfortunately, was not finished at the appointed time, and the prize went to Felicia Hemans, once a fashionable writer, though now forgotten, except perhaps for a stanza that is more often parodied than applauded:

> The stately homes of England!
> How beautiful they stand,
> Amidst their tall ancestral trees,
> O'er all the pleasant land!

However, a member of the Plymouth Chamber of Commerce read Barrington's poem in manuscript, liked it, and arranged for publication. King George IV liked it, too—or was advised that he ought to like it—and accordingly sent the author fifty guineas. Barrington's last poem, *My Native Village*, appeared in 1830, a few months before he died of tuberculosis. 'I have not,' he wrote, 'published any new volume since the publication of *Dartmoor* so many years ago. A severe and protracted illness had prevented me from writing a poem of any length.' He was buried at Combe Hay near Bath, and is remembered at Shaugh Prior, one of his favourite Dartmoor villages, where his name has been inscribed on a rock overlooking the confluence of the Meavy and the Plym.

Approaching Red Lake, the green road veered from west to north-west, through a wilderness of swampy boulders and coarse grass, but still with no sign of bird nor beast. Yet Dartmoor under the Normans was a Royal Forest or hunting ground within the parish of Lydford. In 1239 the forest was granted by Henry III to his brother, Richard, Earl of Cornwall and Poitou, whereupon it lost its royal status, but regained it in 1337 when the King created the Duchy of Cornwall (which included Dartmoor) and then gave it to his heir, the Black Prince. The Sovereign's eldest son is still *ex officio* Duke of Cornwall. As tenants of the Duchy, the medieval monks enjoyed several privileges, some of which have survived, notably 'venville' or the right to graze livestock and to collect heather, stone, sand, peat. The name 'venville' comes from *fin vill*, an abbreviation of *fines villarum*, the fines and rates payable to the Duchy. The rights of venville were vested in twenty-five moorland villages, and could be purchased by all Devon men except the citizens of Barnstaple and Totnes. Dartmoor householders and ratepayers are allowed to burn or swale the heather in order to strengthen its growth by destroying the woody veins. Unfortunately, many moorfolk weaken the growth by burning too often, or when the soil is so dry that the heat withers the roots; and this they do rather as an assertion of privilege than as an improvement of herbage.

By this time the Way was skirting Red Lake, a boggy region, named after the colour of its grass. Beyond Red Lake the track reached 1,500 feet in a wilderness of boulders and brooks. The map showed half a dozen hut circles within a mile of the route. If those hut-dwellers had built more majestically, the region might have been mistaken for one of the cities whose ruin was mourned by the anonymous poet of King Offa's day: '... the old works of the giants stood desolate.' Meanwhile, plodding wearily westward, with a notebook of stale news, I came at last to one of the derelict mines which—almost within living memory—enabled Devon and Cornwall to produce more than half the world's copper. The story of the mines is long and technical. Told briefly, it runs as follows: Bronze Age men obtained metal by sifting and crushing ore from streams. In 1201 King John issued the first Stannary decree (Latin *stannum* or 'tin'), allowing the Devon and Cornish miners to dig without hindrance from landowners. Shaft mining began about the year 1490, and new methods were devised during the Industrial Revolution. Towards the end of the Middle Ages the Dartmoor miners acquired their own Stannary Courts at Ashburton, Chagford, Plympton, and Tavistock, where the production and sale of metal were supervised, and the miners' privileges jealously guarded. From time to time the four Stannary Courts assembled *al fresco* on Crockburn Tor; between 1494 and 1703 ten such assemblies were met. Like some of our trade unions, the miners asserted their own interests without regard for those of other people. They imposed a 'closed shop'. They 'tried' any miner whose conduct or opinion displeased them. Much of their 'justice' was administered and sometimes prematurely executed at Lydford Castle, a prison-like tower, whose walls still stand on a mound beside the parish church. Four centuries ago a Dartmoor poet, William Browne, mocked the miners' Courts:

> I oft have heard of Lydford law,
> How in the morn they hang and draw
> And sit in judgement after . . .
> When I beheld it, Lord, thought I,
> What justice and what clemency . . .

The mining industry suffered a see-saw of booms and crashes. Thus in 1724 Defoe reported: 'The county of Devon has been rich in mines of tin and lead, though they seem at present, wrought out . . . not one tin mine being at work in the whole county.' Between 1780 and 1815 more than twenty-five Dartmoor mines were closed. A revival occurred during the second half of the nineteenth century, but the industry collapsed when Malaya and other distant places began to produce tin cheaply. The derelict shafts now conspire with quarries and china clay sites to create what Jacquetta Hawkes called 'that pervasive sense of degradation which everywhere follows rural mining'.

At Stinger's Hill the track vanished. I therefore proceeded intuitively, trusting that the course would soon reappear as a green albeit rocky road. During the interval I remembered William Crossing, a self-educated antiquary who, like Noel Barrington, deserved more credit than he received. Born at Plymouth in 1847, Crossing became (in Barrington's phrase) 'a highland wanderer' on the moor. Unwilling to work in an office, and unable to write the kind of books that command an adequate income, he passed most of his life in poverty, and three months of it as a pauper at Tavistock workhouse. The barest necessities of married life came to him from local newspapers—*The Devon Evening Express, Mid-Devon and Newton Times, Western Morning News*—which commis-

Almshouses and church at Ewelme

The Icknield Way near Watlington

The old railway station,
Watlington

Thatching near Bledlow

Bignor Hill on Stane Street

Head of Venus: Roman villa, Bignor

Offa's Dyke where it crosses Springhill

Offa's Dyke near Middle Knuck Farm

Clun Castle

Offa's Dyke at Church End, Mainstone

Crossing a stream—Offa's Dyke

Dartmoor Prison

Nun's Cross on the Abbot's Way

A clapper bridge on the Abbot's Way

Buckfast Abbey

The start of the Abbot's Way

sioned him to write articles about Devon in general and Dartmoor in particular. This task enabled him to acquire an unrivalled knowledge of the moor and its people. 'I have,' he claimed, 'made a thorough examination of its prehistoric monuments, such as stone circles, kistvaens, village enclosures, and the like. I have carefully inspected its streamworks and remains of ancient mining operations, its stone crosses, its curious old bridges, and searched out its partially obliterated and forgotten tracks.... Nor have I omitted to jot down incidents connected with the moor which have come before me, and stories of its folklore.' Since local newspapers a century ago seldom paid more than half a guinea for an article, Crossing became so poor that in 1904 a number of west country gentlemen organized an appeal 'to show appreciation of the value of his work; and it is thought that the presentation of a purse would best accomplish this'. Among those who signed the appeal and then subscribed to it were Lord Clifford, Arthur Quiller-Couch, Sabine Baring-Gould, and Eden Phillpotts. But the appeal went almost unheeded, for the nation of the shopkeepers saw no profit to be had from helping an antiquary. The *Western Morning News* announced: 'The wretchedly inadequate nature of the response is a serious reflection on all Westerners.... For some time past, he has been afflicted with illness, and his pen, upon which he is entirely dependent, has been partially laid aside.' Crossing, in fact, was crippled by rheumatism and a broken arm that had never properly set. Fortunately, a Devon landowner, Walter Palmer Collins, came to the rescue by employing him as tutor to his sons. With a sufficient income at last, and ample leisure, Crossing wrote his *Guide to Dartmoor*, a standard work, comparable with Wordsworth's *Guide to the Lakes*, though not, of course, in the same class as literature.

Passing Great Gnats' Head, the Way turned north-east. On the right, in near-mountainous country, stood Plym Head, source of the River Plym (Old English *plym* or 'plum tree'). Did such a tree ever grow at such a height? One doubts it. The river was more likely named after the plum trees along its lower course. Soon a path joined in from the left, linking the Way with a derelict tin mine north-west of Hartor Tors. It seemed an eternity since I had last met a human being. But at that moment, by turning north-west, the Way led me within a mile or so of the ghost of a human being, at a site called Childe's Tomb. If the site had been nearer and less swampy I would have walked there because it recalled a legend about a Plympton man who, dying without issue, decreed that his possessions should pass to the church of the parish in which he was buried. Westcote, the seventeenth-century historian, continued the tale: 'It fortuned that riding forth a-hunting in a cold season, in the forest, he [Childe] casually strayed from his company, and having also lost his way, in long seeking of both he was so benumbed with cold that he was forced to kill his horse and disembowel him and creep into his belly, but that could not preserve him; frozen he was to death, and found by the men of Tavistock, who, with all convenient speed, carried him to be buried in the Abbey.' Despite their speed, Tavistock's men were intercepted by Plympton's. The rest of the legend need not detain us, except to remark that Tavistock and Plympton each claimed the right to bury the body and to receive the reward. That two parish churches should haggle over the body of a dead man may appear unseemly, but, as we have noted, the medieval Church was at least as powerful as a medieval King; and her dignitaries would sometimes invoke the letter of the law even although it meant violating the spirit of the Mass. When Henry II was at his devotions the Abbot of Westminster and the Bishop of Chichester stood within a few feet of the altar, wrangling loudly over a disputed charter. Meantime, the questions remain: did Childe ever exist? Were his person and possessions ever claimed? A twentieth-century scholar, H. P. R. Finberg, discovered records of a tenth-century Devon giant named Childe, whose Will was disputed by Tavistock Abbey. We know, also, that in 1914, on the site of the present Bedford Hotel at Tavistock, a coffin was unearthed containing two skeletons, one of them seven feet tall. Finally, we know that the word 'Childe' comes from the Old English *cild*, a prefix connoting a rich or important person. In short, Childe's Tomb, the site of his death, may confirm the truth of a legend about a very tall man whose body and bequests were disputed by two Dartmoor parishes. A cross was erected on the site in 1812; re-erected in 1890; and again *c.* 1920 by Lieutenant Boyle, RN.

Meanwhile, my notebook repeated its repetitive plaint: 'Utter silence and loneliness' ... 'Now more than 1,400 ft in drizzle and wind' ... 'Getting colder and wilder' ... 'No place for a heart attack' ... 'Still not a sign of birds etc.' In summer, no doubt, I would have seen some sheep, because mutton and fleece are nowadays a staple Dartmoor commodity, though old people can remember when sheep were seldom seen on the moor, unless during summer and in places where they could be easily supervised. In 1910 a Scottish breed was introduced to the northern parts of the moor, where it soon outnumbered the native flocks. Dartmoor's annual sheep-dip takes place in July, when thousands of animals are driven down from the heights by dogs and mounted farmers.

Having failed to see any sheep, I now failed to see any Way. Once again the elusive course had lost itself in a maze of vague paths which may have been trodden by summer sheep. Small wonder that Childe 'lost his way ... frozen he was to death....' Defoe, who may have heard the legend, gave Dartmoor a wide berth, rating it with Exmoor as 'a filthy, barren ground....' Such roads as did serve Devonshire were mere tracks, ill-suited to vehicles. Not even the intrepid Celia Fiennes dared to explore the high moor. 'All their carriages,' she wrote, 'are here of horses with sort of hooks like yoakes upon each side of a good heighth, which are receptacles of their goods ...' Miss Fiennes died in 1741.

Half a century later, in 1791, Coleridge walked through a more civilized corner of the county, from Cullompton to his old home at Ottery St Mary, along a road so atrocious that he cursed it *ex tempore*:

> Revenge and Ire the Poet goad
> To pour his imprecations on the road.

Yet in Coleridge's day the architects were designing some of the most handsome houses that ever have been designed, and during the Middle Ages masons were raising the spire of Salisbury Cathedral and the west front of Wells Cathedral.

Despite the heavy going, I asked myself whether ease of transport is always and everywhere an unmitigated blessing, and whether lack of news is inevitably harmful. Some parts of Dartmoor did not learn of the death of Queen Elizabeth until the Court in London had set aside its long and formal mourning. News of the flight of James II took three months to reach the Orkney crofters. Today, by contrast, every corner of the kingdom is so bombarded by bad news that, like Atlas, even a deep countryman staggers under the weight of the world's misery. Often he is either hardened against it or broken by it. Things that would have roused his ancestors to action leave him unmoved, at any rate in his conscious mind, and he turns to the racing results. In time he ceases even to care that he is powerless to check the insolence of enemies abroad and the sabotage of enemies at home.

Somewhere ahead lay Nun's Cross Farm, but I looked for it in vain. Had I mistaken my bearings? Or lost them? I had certainly under-estimated the extent of wild solitude that still exists in southern England. The Cumbrian fells above Garrigil are higher than Dartmoor; the Northumbrian moors above Alwinton are lonelier; but neither of them is so gauntly oppressive as the Abbot's Way between Huntingdon Cross and Nun's Cross. In short, I was beginning not to enjoy the journey. I therefore sat down on a heap of stones, and fortified myself with food. Ten minutes later I was beginning to enjoy the journey. After all, the drizzle had ceased, the mist was lifting, and, unlike Childe, I had not yet become a bone of contention. For all I knew, I was still on the Abbot's Way, or at least within a few yards of it. Sure enough, the Way soon reappeared as a green road through a level sector, so I strode briskly forward in rhythm with Holst's 'St Paul's Suite', wondering what Nun's Cross Farm would be like. Immersed in those thoughts, I scarcely noticed that the hills were dwindling to hillocks; that the Way was following a stream; that a farmhouse stood on rising ground a mile ahead; and that I must cross a bog in order to reach it. Now a path as it appears on the map does not always resemble a path as it disappears while the pathfinder is trying to follow it. If any monk ever did precede my footsteps through that bog, he assuredly hitched up his habit while crossing. Concerning the farm itself I had received contradictory reports, some saying that it was occupied, others that it was in ruins. From a distance of six hundred yards the house looked empty. At three hundred yards the condition of the roof and walls suggested that it was occupied. At two hundred yards I did not know what to think, because, although the windows were boarded, the garden path had been trodden by recent feet. I later learned that the place served as base for *bona fide* campers. It was certainly a sombre place, two-storeyed and plain, overlooking the rocky desert through which I had passed. One or two trees near the garden emphasized the lack of them elsewhere. Grass grew where flowers once shone, and a wind moaned where voices used to sing. Few sights are more melancholy than a house that has ceased to be a home. At this house the decades of silence seemed to repeat what they had said to Thomas Hardy:

we do not care
Who loved, wept, or died here,
Knew joy, or despair.

William Crossing gave a brief history of Nun's Cross Farm, based on a series of newspaper articles that were published as a book, *Dartmoor Worker*, nearly forty years after his death. 'I can very well remember,' he wrote, 'when John Hooper enclosed the little farm at Nun's Cross, and he told me not long afterwards that by the time he got up his walls and his tiny dwelling, and bought a cow, his limited capital had disappeared, or, as his wife more forcibly put it, he possessed no more than "fourpence ha'penny" to go on with.' Yet Hooper prospered despite the inclement climate and what we now call a lack of amenities. 'During the later part of his life,' Crossing continued, 'he was able to sell £100 worth of cattle yearly, which considering the size of his place was most satisfactory.' The farm, you notice, was 'enclosed' by Hooper, and the enclosure preceded the house. From time immemorial the Duchy tenants were allowed to increase the extent of their holding, so that an heir might lawfully enclose an extra eight acres of moorland if (said Crossing) 'the father and grandfather of the tenant had held the farm successively'. Every such enclosure—called variously land-yoke, landbote, newtake—was marked by stone walls at least four feet high, usually without mortar or turf to bind them. There was, too, a custom whereby a man might lawfully build a house on the moor if the work were done in one day. Since no individual could achieve such a task, the lone builder often enlisted the help of friends, trusting that they would pass unnoticed by the authorities. At Hexworthy the visitors are still shown a cottage which is said to have been built by a man and his friends between sunrise and sunset on the same day.

I spent some time at Nun's Cross Farm, admiring the fortitude of our moorland forefathers. Here were none of those woods and rivers which add colour to the typical English scene; no hedgerows greening in April, no blossom snowing in May; neither church nor tavern nor shop; not even a visible neighbour. The house might have been just another boulder, relic of upheaval and erosion, larger and less jagged than the rest. Yet such houses are not uncommon in mountainous regions. Wordsworth described a similar holding in Westmorland:

> a small hereditary farm.
> An unproductive slip of rugged ground ...
> Sole building on a mountain's dreary edge,
> Remote from view of city spire, or sound
> Of minster clock ...

Like the farmer in Wordsworth's *The Excursion*, John Hooper was a solitary man albeit married:

> He, many an evening, to his distant home
> In solitude returning, saw his hills
> Grow larger in the darkness; all alone
> Beheld the stars come out above his head ...

Did Hooper and his kind dislike the loneliness? Or were they sustained by Wordsworth's 'all-sufficing power of solitude'? No doubt Mrs Hooper took comfort from knowing that the village of Princetown lay only a few miles away; and what were three miles—or six, or ten, or twelve—to the Hoopers of this world? They had no need to hurry. They either walked or rode, and then shopped and gossiped and returned home; and that was that. Things seen or heard by the way—young George's wedding, old Timothy's rheumatism, talk of a tipsy mayor, news of a local bankrupt—all were sampled and digested and regurgitated until, next market day, the cottager went out again, and came back with newer news. True, the blacksmith was *ex officio* the dentist; tramps died of hunger; colliers succumbed to overwork; and persons who took a daily bath were regarded as eccentrics. But true also that at Princetown you could hear the birds; that a penny bought several pipefuls of tobacco; and that England slept peacefully behind her shield of ships.

Nun's Cross Farm stood a few hundred yards off the Way; Nun's Cross stood in the middle of it, a weird apparition, tall as a man whose arms have been partly amputated by the climate. Its original name was Siward's Cross (the Latin equivalent, *Crux Siwardi*, was at one time legibly carved on it). A second inscription, *Boc Lond*, referred to Buckland. Of Siward we know nothing, except that he was a Childe or man of consequence. Of the Cross we know that it was mentioned in a thirteenth-century document, and that it probably marked a boundary of the forest. In short, it was both a topographical and an ecclesiastical relic, though the profane have hinted that it served as rendezvous for unseemly meetings between persons who were sworn to celibacy. Piety, on the other hand, prefers to believe that, if any nuns did walk this Way, they resembled Chaucer's demure virgin:

> Ther was also a Nonne, a Prioresse,
> That of her smyling was ful simple and coy . . .
> She was so charitable and so pitous
> She wolde wepe, if that she saw a mous
> Caught in a trappe . . .

Nun's Cross symbolized the many likenesses, and one outstanding difference, between the Middle and the Atomic Ages. The medieval legacy is more widespread and more varied than that of the Celts, or the Romans, or the Saxons. For example, some men are lords of a manor which their families have held since the Middle Ages; some counties have not changed their border since the Middle Ages; some laws have not been repealed since the Middle Ages. Our unwritten constitution is basically medieval, though universal suffrage has destroyed the balance of power between the Sovereign, the Lords, and the Commons of gentry and well-to-do merchants. In theory we are still governed by 'the Sovereign in Parliament', that is, by the Sovereign co-operating with Parliament; in theory, also, the Sovereign may lawfully reject any Act submitted by Parliament. Many of our national pageants and institutions were devised during the Middle Ages, as, for instance, the form of coronation of a Sovereign and the presentation of the Prince of Wales. The Primate of England and the Primate of All England are medieval creations, as are the Privy Council, the robes and

observances of the judiciary, the Lord Chancellor's Woolsack, the Maundy almsgiving, the Christmas carolling, the
town crier's Oyez, the sounding of curfew at dusk, and in
villages and towns throughout the land a legacy of customs
so numerous that no man has yet recorded all of them, nor is
ever likely to. Above all, Britain is studded with medieval
churches, from the humblest parish to the foremost See.
Some of those churches are decaying; others are redundant;
several have been sold as private houses or as cultural centres.
Britain, in short, is no longer a Christian country; it is a
country with a relatively small percentage of people who
regularly attend a place of Christian worship. But the death
of a religion is not simply the death of a liturgy nor of a
hierarchy. It is the death of an attitude to life itself. Therein
lies the outstanding difference between Nun's Cross and
Leicester Square. That fact would have been anathema to
the monks who made the Abbot's Way. They did not know
that *Homo Sapiens* is a relatively modern creature, still
experimenting with attitudes toward his predicament.

What a difference the sun makes, even on Dartmoor; some
will say, especially on Dartmoor. I once spent a winter there,
when the tors were either swathed in mist or hidden by
rain. Day after day the land unfolded in humps of neutral-
coloured squelchiness; and always it was raining, or about to
rain, or ceasing to rain. Then, one morning in December, the
sun shone from a blue sky; and by its light the tors stood up,
like green mushrooms that had grown overnight. Just such a
sleight-of-light illuminated Nun's Cross at the very moment
when I approached it. As on the clapper bridge, the inter-
lude lasted just long enough for my camera to click. Noel
Barrington witnessed a comparable transformation, and reproduced it with Augustan pomp:

> The welcome Sun
> Chasing the tempest, in the brightening East
> Victorious rose, and through the scatter'd haze
> Brent Tor uplifted his magnific brow . . .

Several streams passed close to Nun's Cross, flowing from Foxtor Mires, a dangerous bog. The last lap of the journey, however, turned north-west, and once again became difficult to follow. On my right a lane from Princetown reached a dead-end at Whiteworks, a derelict industrial site, where kaolin was produced for china clay. The slag-heaps of the trade are worthless, and nobody feels inclined to pay Mammon to remove its own litter. Although I was now within a mile of Princetown, the moor on my right suggested that I was a hundred miles from anywhere. No roads nor houses were visible. Only a few sheep grazed in the foreground, alongside one Dartmoor pony, a mixed and ancient breed, still popular among farmers, and for many years a beast of burden in the coal mines. When electricity replaced horse-power, the ponies ceased to be valuable (I once saw a Dartmoor foal sold for a shilling). Soon after the Second World War the ponies became a status symbol, on which Britons galloped gleefully to the edge of bankruptcy.

Northwards from Whiteworks the solitude was heightened by a dearth of trees. At 800 feet a Dartmoor tree looks wind-worn; at 1,000 feet it struggles for existence; at 1,300 feet it dies. An exception to that rule is Wistman's Wood, near Two Bridges, where four acres of stunted oaks thrive at more than 1,400 feet. The man who first tried to assess their age was Archdeacon Froude, brother of the historian. Having counted 250 rings, the archdeacon gave up because the rest were too indistinct to be identified. Foresters believe that some of the oaks are five centuries old. But why they arose and how they survived is a mystery. A Dartmoor farmer told me that Wistman's Wood took its name from 'wisht', a local word meaning 'eerie'. The Druids, he stated, used to worship there. William Crossing heard the same story, and dismissed it. In any event, Wistman's Wood is out-topped by a moor-land tree at 1,530 feet, which was discovered in 1922 by H. H. Worth, who described it as 'the highest situate in Devonshire ... vigorous and healthy ... pruned remorselessly by the wind ... rising no more than 7 feet 4 inches from the boulders at its base'.

Beyond Nun's Cross the map showed the Way as running parallel with, and only a few yards from, the lane between Whiteworks and Princetown. On each of two journeys, however, I failed to find the Way. On this journey I chose to make a detour along the Princetown lane, in order to peer through the trees at Tor Royal, once the home of Thomas Tyrwhitt, who ranks with the Knights of Exmoor as a resolute reclaimer of stubborn soil. Tyrwhitt was born in 1762, son of an Essex rector. From Eton he went up to Christ Church, Oxford, where he created such a favourable impression that the Dean introduced him to the Prince of Wales, who soon afterwards appointed the youth as his private secretary. In due time Tyrwhitt became auditor of the Duchy of Cornwall, Lord Warden of the Stannaries, Vice-Admiral of Devon and Cornwall, Colonel of the Cornwall Miners' Militia, Member of Parliament, Gentleman Usher of the Black Rod, Knight. At the age of twenty-two he decided to cultivate some of the bleakest parts of Dartmoor: 'To reclaim,' as he put it, 'and clothe with grain and grasses, a spacious tract of land now lying barren and neglected; to fill this unoccupied space with an industrious and hardy population.' The population itself, which was as hardy as any in Britain, predicted failure. But Tyrwhitt remained undeterred. Leasing a thousand acres from the Duchy, he built a village, naming it Prince's Town as a compliment to his royal master. Cottages sprang up, a mill, an inn, and a toll house to finance new roads. Tyrwhitt's own house was set on the outskirts of the village, and again he paid a compliment by naming the place Tor Royal. Completed in 1798, the house received an extra wing in 1815, and was restored by Sir Albert Richardson a century later. Despite his manifold duties, Tyrwhitt personally planned and supervised the campaign against a hostile region. To serve the tin and copper mines, he laid twenty-three miles of horse tramway, including the world's first railroad tunnel, 620 yards long. He

planted hemp and flax. He founded Prince's Town market,
hoping to encourage the sale of local produce. But in the
end he failed, as the moorfolk had foretold, defeated by the
climate and the soil. His cottages stood empty; the mill was
idle; the inn lacked customers. That Prince's Town survived at all was due to Tyrwhitt's best-known achievement, a
prison.

It is a pity that men's attempt to save Time has corrupted
the proper names of so many places. Prince's Town, for instance, is now called Princetown. Yet if you spoke and wrote
the abbreviation a hundred times a day for a hundred years,
I doubt that you would save more than a few minutes and
one bottle of ink. On the edge of Princetown I climbed a knoll
overlooking the Way I had come. To the monks, no doubt,
the Way was neither much more nor much less hazardous
than any other medieval road. Indeed, the best parts of it
were at least as good as some of the nineteenth-century
roads which Baring-Gould described: 'I have,' he wrote, 'a
coachman who has been in the family for seventy-five years.
This old man remembers the state of the country before
most of the new roads were made. Formerly the roads were
not exactly paved, but were made by the thrusting of big
stones into holes which they more or less adequately filled.
Then on top of all were put smaller stones picked up from
the fields, and not broken at all.' Baring-Gould disliked the
lane that passed the gate to his estate at Lew Trenchard:
'The floor is a series of rocky steps, and I can recall when
these steps were eased to the traveller by the heaping of
boulders upon them producing a rude slope. But as with
heavy rain a rush of water went down this road, it dislodged
the boulders, and woe betide the horse descending the steep
declivity of loosely distributed rolling stones on an irregular
and fragile stair of slate.' The writer of those words did not
die until 1924, fifteen centuries after the Romans had built
Stane Street. Moreover, the Romans themselves ventured
into Devon, even onto Dartmoor. Give or take a few miles,
therefore, I could repeat Masefield's statement of fact:

Here the legion halted, here the ranks were broken,
And the men fell out to gather wood;
And the green wood smoked, and bitter words were spoken,
And the trumpets called to food.

While I was standing on the knoll a drizzle set in, so I walked to Princetown, where everyone had retired indoors. At all times the village looks grey and unlovely; seen through rain, it now appeared desolate. The empty shops displayed picture postcards, ice-cream, brassy bric-à-brac, and other attractions for tourists who stare at the prison on a hillside at the edge of the village. Tyrwhitt built Dartmoor Prison in an attempt to revive his dying Town by accommodating French prisoners during the Napoleonic war. He did not intend to accommodate criminals. The Prince of Wales, as Duke of Cornwall, not only approved the scheme but also granted 380 acres for 99 years, and promised to build a chapel at his own cost. In 1806 Tyrwhitt laid the foundation stone of a building arranged in five blocks, like the spokes of a wheel, each holding 1,590 men, who slept in hammocks. The top storey was used for exercise during bad weather. Villagers were admitted, to sell their produce to any prisoner who could afford to buy it. In 1812, when America declared war on England, the prison received 250 Americans who, with the French, helped to build the Prince's chapel, now the parish church. At the end of hostilities the prisoners returned home, leaving the prison as a grey elephant. In 1818 a Committee of the House of Commons agreed that the premises might be used as a School of Industry for training poor children. Several years later the infirmary was rented by a company which tried and failed to produce naphtha gas from peat. In 1842, at the suggestion of the Prince Consort, the prison became a penal settlement. Twenty-one years later Murray's *Handbook to Devon and Cornwall* announced: 'More than 100 acres around the prison are now under tillage, and produce abundant crops of mangle-wurzles, carrots, barley, oats, flax, and vetch.'

Visitors were allowed to inspect the premises: 'For seeing the prison an order (readily procured) from the Home Office is necessary.'

Known to its inmates as 'The Moor', the present prison is a single block, flanked by workshops and outbuildings, with a wide and often weary view of distant tors. For many years the warders rode Dartmoor ponies while supervising convicts in the fields, or trying to capture them when they had escaped; but in 1974 the ponies were replaced by cars in an effort to keep pace with progress. The French and Americans would have envied the more humane treatment accorded to criminals: television and radio, hot baths, varied diet, weekly wages, library and lectures, organized games, visits from relatives, and a hostel for those relatives (built partly by warders gratis in their leisure time).

From high ground beyond the village I looked once more along the Way I had come, with the mind's eye imagining Nun's Cross Farm and Huntingdon Warren, Childe's Tomb and the rocky desolation, the clapper bridge and Buckfast Abbey. The medieval monks certainly planned their own journeys with due regard for the hour and the weather, yet many of them encountered a mist or a blizzard, and some fell by the Way, never to rise. What changes the earlier abbey had witnessed; not, indeed, the radical changes of our own era, but rather a series of subtle innovations. When Buckfast Abbey was founded, the inhabitants of England were Christians rather than Europeans; and Normans, or Northumbrians, or East Anglians rather than Englishmen. The Dartmoor dialect sounded as strange in Sussex as in Shropshire. But when Buckfast Abbey was dissolved, the inhabitants of England were Protestants rather than Christians, and English rather than European. Their speech was understood in every county, except by a small number of people who spoke only the Cornish tongue. It is true that the peasant still looked to his lord, and seldom ventured far beyond his manor; yet Henry V had long since cried: 'God for Harry, England, and Saint George!' The girl had already been born who, as Queen Elizabeth, would one day send a challenge to the Spanish Armada: 'I know I have the body of a weak and feeble woman, but I have the heart and stomach of a king, and of a king of England too, and think it foul scorn that Parma or Spain, or any prince of Europe, should dare to invade the borders of my realm.'

When the last pre-Reformation monk walked the Abbot's Way, the majority of erstwhile Celts and Saxons and Angles and Vikings and Normans could with one voice anticipate William Cowper's critical allegiance:

England, with all thy faults, I love thee still.

A Scottish Drove Road

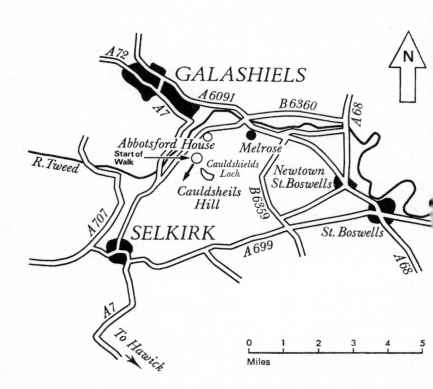

6 A Scottish Drove Road

T HE sky was loud with larks. I had never before heard so many, seen so many. Each singer harmonized with the rest, achieving the resonance which Charles Wesley likened to a worldwide carillon:

Hark how all the welkin rings . . .

Once again I marvelled at my good luck, for I had travelled five hundred miles, trusting that April would smile between the showers, and, lo, the sun shone from a cloudless sky.

The time was noon; the place, a green road through Selkirkshire in the Scottish Lowlands, a term misleading to anyone who interprets it as 'lowlying'. The Lowlands are hilly, and their name was intended to distinguish them from the mountainous parts of central and western Scotland. As for the green road, I had discovered it by chance while visiting Abbotsford, Sir Walter Scott's home, three miles west of Melrose, where they told me that a drove road lay within a short distance. This information cut short my literary pilgrimage, offering instead a journey over the hills and far away. Nevertheless, I did spend some time at Scott's home, a mansion in the baronial style, towered and turreted, a poet's romantic recreation of medieval noblesse, set in a land of farms and little else, dominated by the Eildon Hills. Scott's descendants maintain their heritage by opening it to the public. There I saw his book-lined study, with his pens and spectacles on the desk. Of the many other heirlooms, I remember 'Bonnie' Prince Charles's drinking cup, Burns's tumbler, and the desk and chairs that were a gift from George IV. I could have spent several hours at Abbotsford, but the clock was striking eleven, and the weather persuaded me to move from the past to the present, following a lane which Scott himself had followed while he rode on the crest of a wave that took shape in 1805, when he published a successful verse-novel, *The Lay of the Last Minstrel*. Some years later, having bought a farm, he demolished the farmhouse, and on the site erected a mansion, naming it Abbotsford because the land once belonged to Melrose Abbey. At Abbotsford he achieved fame, fortune, a baronetcy; and there, at the height of his career, he was ruined by the failure of a publishing firm in which he had invested huge sums of money. So, the rich laird became a penniless bankrupt. Partly from self-interest, however, and partly from deference to a national figure, his creditors allowed him to remain at Abbotsford, believing that he was an honourable man, eager to make reparation. They were not mistaken. Scott produced a spate of poetry, fiction, and biography; year after year labouring so heroically that the debt was repaid, though at some cost to his health and his artistry.

By this time the lane had acquired a grass parting down the middle, and was deeply rutted. 'You can park the car,' they had told me, 'beside a barn.' Halting to check my position, I found that I was on a hill, overlooked by higher hills to the left, all of them domed, treeless, sheep-speckled. On the right lay a wood, and in the depths of it a stretch of shining water. Ahead were more hills, likewise sheep-speckled, treeless, domed; and over them ran a track that grew greener as it climbed.

The barn proved to be an unsightly building, surrounded by old sacks, old hay, old tyres. Farmers are indeed conservationists. Just short of the barn, on the left, Cauldshields Loch winked a blue eye. Compared with the Highland lochs it was no more than a large pond, yet Scott fondly rated it above the beautiful Loch Coruisk on Skye, dismissing the latter as 'a sheet of water which, though recommended by Macleod of Macleod, does not equal even Cauldshiels Loch'. Having parked the car, the dog and I proceeded on foot. The day being hot, and the road green, I walked naturally, which is to say shoeless and without socks. Presently I passed a sheep-dip that had been concocted of concrete and some brown painted panelling from a hideous room. Beyond the sheep-dip, on the right, two black horses sunbathed full-length, watched by some Friesians and twelve Cheviots. At first the road climbed gently, accompanied on the left by a stone wall; but the gradient soon stiffened, and the high ground on my right gave way, revealing a wide valley wherein two farmsteads sheltered in a circle of wind-breaking conifers. Many Scottish plantations are relatively modern. In 1705, for example, Lord Hamilton planted 800 acres of pine. In 1716 Sir Alexander Grant began a famous process whereby, at the end of a long life, he had planted millions of trees on his land. In 1736 prizes were awarded, to encourage Scottish farmers to plant oak and ash and elm.

Near the brow of the first slope I glanced back, like a sailor taking his last look at the land astern. There lay the green road, the sheep-dip, the barn, the car, the loch. From the brow of the second slope I glanced back again, but this time saw only the brow of the previous slope. It was as though I had reached a gigantic golf course, whose hazards were hills. On the left, less than a mile away, Cauldshields Hill stood a thousand feet among the larks. The sides of the hill were grazed by sheep which, seen from a distance, might have been mountain hares in their winter coats. For another quarter-mile the road climbed in a wide arc, still accompanied by the stone wall; and in the lee of that wall crouched a thorn tree, patiently awaiting the late flowering of its leaves. Like the oaks in Wistman's Wood on Dartmoor, the thorn was gnarled and stunted, though still far below the tree-limit in Britain, which exceeds two thousand feet, and is reached by the pines at Creag Phialiach among the Cairngorms. Defoe offered some advice to windswept lairds: 'Trees,' he informed them, 'should all be secur'd by a triangular frame to each tree; that is to say, three large stakes set about them in an equilateral triangle, and fasten'd all together by three short cross pieces at the top; and these stakes should stand from 7 to 8 feet high. In the centre of the triangle stands the planted tree; which way soever the wind blows, the body bends from it to the cross-piece, which joins the stake to that side, and which makes the triangle, by which means the root is not shaken, or the earth mov'd and loosen'd about it, and then the tree will strike root, and grow, and grow.' Lacking such support, a sapling is likely to die because, as Defoe pointed out, 'the winds, especially in winter, being very strong in that country, the tree is bended every way, and the earth loosen'd continually about it, and the root is often stirred, and the tree gets no time to strike root into the earth. And this is why in many of the gentlemen's parks, I saw trees stented and bauk'd.'

Beyond the second slope the road reached a comparatively level sector, wide as a country lane. The turf had long ago been darkened by the passage of drovers, mighty men, strong-limbed, light-hearted, and so canny that few of them were ever outwitted by a Smithfield dealer. George Borrow painted an unfavourable portrait of a drover, presenting him as idle and dishonest. Shakespeare, on the other hand, made Benedick exclaim: 'Well, that's spoke like an honest drovier....' No doubt some double-dealing did occur. No doubt, either, that those who practised it were ultimately detected and dismissed. Many of the drovers acted as agents for people wishing to do business in London, or Edinburgh, or Carlisle. During the eighteenth century the drovers were required to carry an official licence as evidence of their integrity. All drovers went armed against robbers, with their cattle divided into herds of two hundred apiece, each herd controlled by a horseman and his dog. Sheep travelled faster than cattle, and could cover more than a dozen miles a day. At night the animals were usually quartered in wayside fields, for which the farmer charged anything from a farthing to a penny per head, as in James Gurney's childhood beside the Icknield Way.

English prosperity was founded on fleece. As a symbol of

that fact, the Lord Chancellor sits on a woolsack when pre-
siding over the House of Lords. Medieval wool merchants
formed the first English trading company, the Fellowship of
the Merchants of the Staple, which for three centuries remained our foremost commercial organization, administering the collection and sale of wool. At first the wool was exported as a raw commodity, but when the French and
Flemish weavers migrated to England the wool was often
sold as cloth. In 1454 the House of Commons declared:
'The making of cloth within all parts of the realm is the
greatest occupation and living of the poor commons of this
land.' In 1660 they said the same thing in different words;
asserting that the woollen textile industry was 'the principal
foundation upon which the foreign commerce of this kingdom moveth'. Sheep became of prime importance when the
Black Death killed so many peasants that wages soared with
the scarcity of labour. As a result, vast areas of arable land
were set to pasture because one shepherd could tend many
sheep. In his book about an ideal State, *Utopia*, Sir Thomas
More mocked the process whereby England was placing most
of her eggs in a single Continental wool basket: 'Your
sheape,' he cried, 'that were wont to be so meke and tame,
and so smal eaters, now as I hear say, become so great
devowrers and so wylde, that they eate up, and swallow
downe the very men themselfes. They consume, they de-
stroye, and devoure whole fields, howses, and cities....' At
one time, indeed, wool represented more than three-quarters
of all exports from England and Wales. Milton, therefore,
was citing a social convention, not an economic decline, when
he spoke of 'the homely shepherd's slighted trade'.

Droving reached its zenith during the eighteenth and early
nineteenth centuries, a time of expanding industry, rising
population, and increasing demand for both fleece and food.
From Lincolnshire alone some 20,000 geese were driven
each year to Nottingham's Michaelmas Goose Fair. In 1745
a Yorkshireman, John Birtwhistle of Malham, had ten thousand animals on the drove roads from Scotland. Mr Jorrocks

once encountered 'large droves of Scotch kyloes.... There might be fifty or sixty of them, duns, browns, mottles, reds, and blacks, with wildness depicted in the prominent eyes of the broad faces'. Passing a Yorkshire tavern, the Hon. John Byng noticed that the adjacent field was 'crowded with Scotch cattle and drovers; and the house cramm'd by buyers and sellers, most of whom were in plaids'. Defoe remarked: 'It is no uncommon thing for a Galloway nobleman to send 4,000 sheep and 4,000 head of black cattle to England in a year, and sometimes much more.'

The next summit was higher than the others, so for a third time I looked back, wondering whether I might see Cauldshields Loch; but only the hills were visible, and the green road disappearing round a bend near the thorn tree. Had that tree stood there when Scott passed by? Few people, I reflected, now read his prose, partly because novels are difficult to carry from one century to another. A lyric poem, on the other hand, travels light, and is likely to transcend the fashion. The best of Scott's lyrics are stripped of ornamentation:

> Proud Maisie is in the wood,
> Walking so early;
> Sweet robin sits on the bush
> Singing so rarely....

Still the road climbed, this time with a row of trees on the right, all bent by the wind, and none equipped with Defoe's triangle. It was there that I lay in the sun, hearing the larks while the stone wall shielded me from the breeze. For the first time since September I felt really warm. In fact, I removed my shirt. While I was doing so, the dog began to growl. Glancing up, I sighted an old man walking downhill at a brisk pace, followed by his Border collie. It was as well that I went out to meet him, because he had turned towards the valley before I came alongside. We got talking, chiefly about Cheviots and organic farming, both of which he admired. Like Wordsworth's leech-gatherer, the shepherd used

> Choice words, and measured phrase, above the reach
> Of ordinary men; a stately speech;
> Such as grave livers do in Scotland use.

Too courteous to sound inquisitive, the Scot phrased his question as a statement: 'You are, no doubt, walking for pleasure.'

'For pleasure,' I assented.

'Ye'll no' reach Hawick afoor teatime.'

I replied that I had no intention of reaching Hawick, neither before teatime nor after. The shepherd seemed disappointed. 'But,' he said, 'you *could* reach it.'

'On this road?'

'Why not? 'Tis a guid green gait.'

'A good green road indeed. In fact, a drove road.'

'But only for a few miles. Flocks travel by lorry now. Yon's no' been a busy road since great-grandfather's day. Jock o' the Shiels they called him. He really did drive sheep. Aye, and he'd take your money to the Bank o' London if you tipped him. He came this way to Caril.'

'Carlisle?'

'Aye, Caril. And then he followed th'auld Scotch gait o'er the fells to Kairby Lonsdale.'

'Quite a stroll.'

'I'd no' care to do it mesel'. I have been young, and now am old.' He quizzed me. 'Ye ken your Bible, I trust? Weel, ken or no', I'm past seventy at last, and when I've walked twelve miles I like to lie-up awhile.'

'Have you far to go?'

'Yon valley.' He pointed in the direction of Galashiels, which lay behind the hills. 'There's a party waiting to gie us a lift.' This time he pointed to Abbotsford, again posing his question as a statement: 'I'm thinking ye'll hae' seen Abbotsford.'

'I have indeed.'

'A grand old gentleman, Sir Walter. They say the whole

kingdom grieved when he died. Aye, and the London news-papers carried a black border.'

'Yes, a form of mourning usually reserved for kings.'

'Sir Walter was a laird. And a laird *is* a king, or used to be. In those years we were Scotland. Today we're a peep-show for tourists. I've heard it's just as bad in England.'

'It's worse.'

'And there's ne'er a sign of it mending. But I bide at home, thank God, where a man belongs.' Now it was the sun he glanced at. 'Come, collie. Mother will hae' the pot boiling, and we've still a way to gang.' The collie came to heel. 'So I'll wish ye guid day, Mister.' Once more he paused, this time staring at my shirtless shoulders, after which—with another glance at the beaming sun—he removed his jacket, and then strode away, four miles an hour through a grass ocean.

The sight of the tweed jacket slung over his arm re-minded me that Galashiels was a pioneer among Scottish wool traders, with a Weavers' Corporation of 1666 and a Manufacturers' Corporation of 1777. Despite its fame, how-ever, the word 'tweed' is a misnomer, which seems to have been perpetrated by an Englishman who supposed that the old Scots 'tweel' or twill ought to have been 'tweed' because most of the local woollen garments were made in the Tweed Valley. The cloth itself is distinguished by parallel diagonal ridges which are produced by passing the weft threads over one and then under two or more of the warp threads, where-as in plain weaving the thread is passed over and under in regular sequence. The Scottish tweed industry owed much to a London shopkeeper, John Locke, who in 1830 or there-abouts invented the pattern book, thereby enabling a com-mercial traveller to carry many samples in a small space.

Before continuing my journey, I took a last look at the shepherd, who now seemed as dim as a dot. Our encounter had heightened what we call solitude, that is, an absence of other human beings. In reality, of course, I was not alone. Overhead, the larks abounded; all around, the sheep shone like wool-wisps; underfoot, the soil teemed with bacteria. Microbes, after all, are more numerous than men; rabbits are more prolific, flowers are more peaceable, and sponges are more contented. The road meanwhile climbed steadily, but without bringing me noticeably nearer to the next summit, though I walked at four miles an hour. How elusive the summit must have seemed to drovers ambling at two miles an hour. What a lathering of horses while they galloped up and down the line, goading the dawdlers or chasing the strays; what a lolling of tongues by thirsty dogs; what a thudding of hooves, and bleating of sheep, and lowing of cattle. You could have heard them a mile away ... the shouts, barks, whistles, oaths. Nor was the procession a rare event, watched only by hilltop hinds. It was a continuous tide. Even in winter it flowed, sometimes reaching London, at other times ending at a Lowland farm or in a Northumbrian market. Like ships at sea, the passing travellers exchanged news: 'Fergus fell and broke his neck in Kendal' ... 'The King died last week' ... 'A miser at York offered less than it cost me to feed 'em' ... 'There's six foot o' snow t'other side o' Hawick' ... 'Smithfield's paying a bonnie price this month' ... 'Watch out for Mollie's husband at the Woolpack.' Sometimes the drover returned with a long face and an empty purse. Robbers may have waylaid him; rustlers may have killed one of his mates; plague may have infected the herd; the market may have forced him to sell at a loss. In 1618, for example, Lincolnshire merchants were buying wool at fourteen shillings per stone, yet in 1621 the price had dropped by twenty-five per cent.

On, then, into solitude and birdsong, along a road that appeared to have cast away all sadness. But then I noticed the bones of a lamb whose birth and death went unnoticed except by its mother and the crows. The bleached relics reminded me of the sombre verdicts of the three other men whose ghosts had walked along the green roads of Britain: Hilaire Belloc of Stane Street, who said: 'Of all creatures that move upon the earth we of mankind are the fullest of sorrows'; Edward Thomas of Icknield Way, who said : 'I am weary of everything ... There is nothing else in my world but my dead heart and brain'; and Sir Walter Scott of Abbotsford, who said : 'Death is the perfect freedom.'

Immersed in the mystery of genes and genius, I almost failed to notice that the road had dipped slightly, and was approaching a copse on the left, dwarfed by a radio mast, tall as the antenna of a monstrous insect. If the mast was broadcasting wars or the rumours thereof, that would have seemed no novelty in these parts, a no-man's-land stained with blood. The Border wars between England and Scotland were a blend of national campaign and private feud, continuing throughout the Middle Ages, and not ceasing until the Jacobite Rising of 1745, nearly half a century after the formal Act of Union. The last battle yet fought on English soil occurred in 1745 at Clifton in Westmorland, where the King's army attacked a party of retreating Jacobites. The most famous of the national campaigns occurred in 1513, when the Scottish King, having invaded England, was killed at Flodden Field, alongside the flower of his nobility and gentry. Thirty years later the English were still erecting defences against the Scots. An Order in Council decreed that 'all havens should be fenced with bulwarks and bloke houses against the Scots'. As a result, Holy Island Castle was built, to guard Northumberland from seaborne invasion. The private feuds were a blend of murder and looting. The most famous of them occurred when the Scottish Earl Douglas plundered Northumberland, and was pursued and attacked by his old enemy, Sir Henry Percy, at the Battle of Chevy Chase near Otterburn. History shows that the Scots looted more frequently than the English. They razed churches, burned castles, destroyed villages, killed peasants. But the English, too, could be barbarous. As Scott's Minstrel remarked, the neighbouring kingdoms were

> By mutual inroads, mutual blows,
> By habit, and by nation, foes....

The one good thing that did emerge from those wars was a legacy of poems, commonly called the Border Ballads, composed for the most part by anonymous Scotsmen and Englishmen. Varying in length, metre, merit, and theme, the ballads were devised for the people and by the people and about the people. Many of the Scottish ballads open with a gleeful call to arms:

> Fair Johnnie Armstrong to Willie did say
> 'Billie, a riding we will gae;
> England and us have long been at feud;
> Perhaps we'll light on some bootie.'

The anonymous ballad-makers were not great poets, but they did possess a flair for narrative, and sometimes they rang the deepest bell:

> Oh, little did my mother think,
> The day she cradled me,
> What lands I was to travel through,
> What death I was to dee.

From the end of the Middle Ages until the end of the eighteenth century the ballads were bequeathed orally. Of those that had been written down, several were preserved by a Shropshire man, Thomas Percy, sometime Dean of Carlisle and Bishop of Dromore, who rescued a sheaf of manuscript poems which a fellow-Salopian was using as fire-lighters. In 1765 Percy published a collection of the poems, *The Reliques of English poetry: Old Heroic Ballads, Songs and Other Pieces, of our Earlier Poetry (chiefly of the lyric kind)*. This was the anthology that first opened Scott's eyes to the legacy of both nations: 'Nor do I believe,' he confessed, 'I ever read a book half so frequently, or with half such enthusiasm.' He was later to enrich the legacy with his own *Minstrelsy of the Scottish Border*. Scott loved England and the English; not, of course, as dearly as he loved Scotland and the Scots, yet with chivalry that emphasized his ultimate allegiance to the United Kingdom.

Addison said that the Border ballads were the favourite literature of the common people, who sang them round the fire at night; a statement which Thomas Bewick confirmed by recalling the winter evenings of his own Northumbrian childhood 'spent in listening to the traditional tales and songs, relating to men who had been eminent for their prowess and bravery in the border wars ...' The common people have now forgotten these songs, or never knew them, and either way feel no desire to sing them. The danger was foreseen by Mrs Hogg, mother of a Lowland shepherd, who told Scott that he had killed the ballads by 'prenting 'em in a bewk. There never war one o' my sangs prentit till ye prentit them yoursel', an' ye have spoilt them awthergither. There were made for singing an' they'll never be sang mair.'

How far had Scott himself travelled on this green road? Did he ride here on 22 January 1826, when he knew that he was bankrupt, but did not know that his creditors would allow him to remain at Abbotsford? 'I have walked,' he wrote in his *Journal*, 'my last on the domains I have planted—sate the last time in the halls I have built ... I find my eyes moistening, and that will not do.' Then spake the man within the man: 'I will not yield without a fight for it.' Nor did he yield. Already, on that January evening, he had fired the first salvo: 'It is odd, when I set myself to work *doggedly*, as Dr Johnson would say, I am exactly the same man that I ever was, neither low-spirited nor *distrait*. In prosperous times I have some-times felt my fancy and powers of language flagging, but adversity is to me at least a tonic and a bracer; the fountain is awakened from its inmost recesses.' Some years later, weary after a long day at his desk, he made a brief and moving entry in the *Journal*: 'Well done, Sir Walter Scott.' Yet Abbotsford contributed nothing to his art. Neither the house nor the estate appear in his books. Scott's inspiration came from Edinburgh, Liddesdale, and England ('England,' he told Surtees, 'made me what I am'). Abbotsford, by contrast, merely aggravated his ambition to live like a medieval laird. He triumphed despite that ambition, not because of it. Nevertheless, the Eildon Hills and the River Tweed must surely have refreshed him in his labours. Myself, I tried to see the green road as Scott had seen it. The pylon, of course, appeared after his death, and so had the barn, the two farmhouses in the valley, and perhaps the stone wall; but the rest had scarcely changed, because the rest was sheep and hills. I saw them wherever I looked. There was little else to see; just blue sky, green hills, white sheep, and the road itself, dark green on pale green, rising and falling, swerving and straightening, widening and narrowing.

The going was so good, and the sun so warm, that I felt able to walk until twilight, all the while aware of being an alien, that is, *alienus* or 'a visitor from another country', for Scotland is indeed not England. Strathclyde was anciently a Welsh settlement; Orkney and Caithness were Norwegian territory throughout the Middle Ages; and Dalriada was founded by Irishmen, whence the saying that Ireland is 'the ancient and greater Scotland' (*vetus et major Scotia*). Scotland has its own Kirk, its own law, and its own language, the Gaelic, which in various forms and until the eighteenth century was spoken throughout Scotland, Ireland, and the Isle of Man. Boswell, however, detected a falling-off: 'The great, the learned, the ambitious, and the vain,' he wrote, 'all cultivate the English phrase and the English pronunciation, and in splendid company Scotch is not much heard, except now and then from an old lady.' But the decline began long before Boswell's day. In 1559 John Knox boasted to Mary Queen of Scots that the congregation at Ayr had mistaken him for an Englishman. Hindsight may regret the magnetism of London, but only *naiveté* will blame those who succumbed to it. London, after all, was the centre of government and culture and commerce. Four centuries ago a Scottish poet, William Dunbar, fell under its spell:

> London, thou art the flower of cities all!
> Gemme of all joy, jasper of jocunditie.

James First and Sixth spoke with a broad Scots accent; not so the Georgian and Victorian lairds, many of whom had learned their accent on the playing fields of England. Attendance at the House of Lords ensured that both the Welsh and the Scottish nobility would ultimately be anglicized. Patriotism in modern England has fallen from favour, at any rate among the rootless intellectuals. Almost everywhere else, by contrast, it is very much in the vogue, especially among people who suppose that a love of one's country implies a hatred of somebody else's. Like charity, patriotism begins at home, and 'home' means something more than a political régime. It means one's kith and kin, and the best traditions of one's ancestors, and the landscape which they laboured to create. If a man does hate his homeland, it is unlikely that he will love anyone else's; at most he will prefer its political régime. Tudor England was by no means a Welfare State, yet one of its common people—a man named Shakespeare—scorned the Englishman who hates England. Such a renegade, he said, is forever belittling 'all the benefits of his own country, out of love with his nativity'. Again like charity, patriotism does not end at home, for if a man fails to love other lands he will never succeed in loving his own; he will merely be infatuated by it, blind to its defects, and blind also to the merits of other nations. As an Englishman in Scotland, therefore, I uttered an ancient boast: 'What land is more beautiful than Scotland?' (*Tecum Scotia nostra comparatur*).

Beauty, alas, was ever a fragile commodity; and the boast therefore implied a question: 'Whither Scotland?' In 1776 the Scottish population represented sixteen per cent of the British population; in 1976, only ten per cent. Again it was Boswell who noted the decline: 'Emigration was at this time the common topick of conversation.' During the second half of the nineteenth century some half a million Scots emigrated; during the first half of the twentieth century the number of emigrants exceeded a million. The reason for that exodus may fairly be summarized as the callous greed of the

Scottish lairds and the industrial bias of the British weather-vane, which drove the reluctant crofters to seek new pastures in distant lands or to live in a strange urban air. Scotland to-day is still chiefly farmland, and large tracts of it are so in-clement that only eagles and rocks can thrive there; yet forty per cent of the Scottish population now live in four cities, Edinburgh, Glasgow, Aberdeen, Dundee. Moreover, since those cities are industrial, they rely on non-Scottish investors, few of whom are likely to be impressed by Gaelic news-papers, Scottish parliaments, and a kilted ambassador at the Disunited Nations. Whether we like it or not, the economy and defence of Scotland and Wales would collapse if the English taxpayers ceased to subsidize them. But Scottish nationalism is a flower so hardy that it ought to look with scorn on bilingual signposts and other archaic gew-gaws. Above all, it must beware the international greed of North Sea oil and Come-Again-Tourism. The true symbols of Scottish nationalism are the Queen (a Royal Scot), the Kirk, the Gaelic, the Border ballads, the pibroch, the islands, the bens and the braes and the lochs. There beats the heart of Scotland, the Land of the Immortals, *Tir nan Og*. If that kind of nationalism remains true to itself, Scotland will be flourishing when England has withered into a multi-racial hotch-potch of redundant factory hands. Scott knew so and said so, in words that mention neither votes nor money:

> Land of the heath and shaggy wood,
> Land of the mountains and the flood,
> Land of my sires.

Through that land I could indeed have walked until twi-light; but had I done so I might have found myself hungry and bedless on a hill among hills. So, I went back, following the same road while seeing the world from a different angle; a world at peace, though formerly a battlefield. Only a few miles to the north lay Galashiels, whose motto—Sour Plums —recalled a medieval Border skirmish wherein the towns-folk slew some English raiders who were stealing plums. In

1409 Jedburgh destroyed its own castle lest the English took it as a base. Scarcely two miles beyond Abbotsford lay Melrose, whose Cistercian abbey was razed by the English in 1524. Hawick flaunted a Horse Monument in memory of local callants or youths who fought the English in 1514. And Selkirk claimed to possess an English banner that was captured by local soutars or shoemakers at Flodden Field.

Presently the pylon reappeared, this time on my right; then the stone wall; then the solitary thorn; each simmering in sunlight. I hoped that the old shepherd had enjoyed his midday meal, and was now at ease in a chair beside the porch. At the thorn tree I rested awhile, not for my own sake but for the dog's; he being then in his fourteenth year, a Lakeland terrier and therefore indomitable. 'April,' said T. S. Eliot, 'is the cruellest month ...' For me, April had proved the kindest month, distilling the attar of spring and a foretaste of summer.

At the very moment when I was imagining the road in its heyday, teeming with sheep, I heard the sound of a flock on the march, accompanied by barking dogs, shouting men, thudding hooves. It seemed too good to be true, yet true it was, visible and audible as I hurried forward to the next summit; and there, surging up the hill, were the handsomest of all sheep, the Cheviots, with dainty feet and delicately-pointed features; a breed able to graze their living in climates and altitudes that would starve most other flocks. Sometimes called the Great Sheep, Cheviots were imported from England during the eighteenth century. In 1790 they travelled as far north as the Cromarty Firth. In 1792 Sir John Sinclair of Ulbster took them to Caithness. Within a few years the pastures that had produced 2d an acre under cattle were producing 2s an acre under Cheviots. The best Scottish tweeds are woven of Cheviot wool, and the old shepherd could remember the years when Cheviots and Suffolks took more Smithfield prizes than did all the other breeds combined.

There was no time for gossip as the flocks passed by. Wide

though it seemed, the road bulged with sheep, some trotting, some dawdling, some trying to browse while they were jostled onward. Two Border collies raced round the flanks, swift as destroyers escorting a convoy. Once or twice a horseman called to them, and away they went, heading-off a stray, barking-on a straggler. The green road had come alive, as in the years when sheep spun their golden fleece from Cornwall to Caithness. We all waved in passing, and then they were gone, growing fainter and smaller until, near the next summit, they headed into the hills.

A few minutes later I sighted the sheep-dip and after that the car, glinting like a lighthouse. Still the larks sang, and the loch winked, and the livestock grazed. Men had not yet learned to live by factories alone. Food came first, from farming; a peaceable occupation, exercising the body, and in many ways enriching the mind. If Sir Walter Scott were alive today, I thought, he would agree that the winding green road had scarcely changed since he was laird of Abbotsford:

> Where'er thou wind'st, by dale or hill,
> All, all is peaceful, all is still . . .

The Kennet and Avon Canal

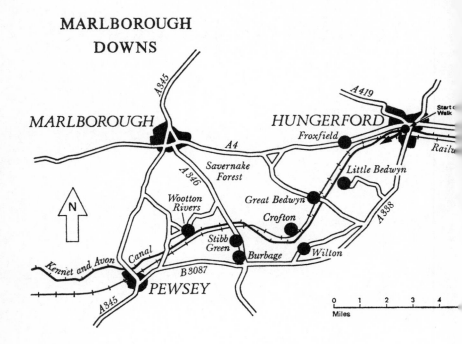

7 The Kennet and Avon Canal

THE road was as green as grass could make it, yet narrow enough for me to lie full-length across it, basking in autumn sunshine while ducks ruffled the water within a yard of my feet, and crows pecked the furrows within a yard of my head. The only sound was a robin's song. Soon even the song ceased, and utter stillness returned to the Kennet and Avon Canal.

I had joined the canal at Hungerford, a steep and handsome town on the River Kennet in Berkshire; nowadays a well-fed town, though its name means 'ford where people are hungry'. The Kennet itself has long been an angler's paradise. Six hundred years ago John of Gaunt granted fishing rights to ninety-nine householders or Tuttimen, whose successors still assemble on Tuesday in Easter Week, to parade their titties or nosegays; to claim kisses from the ladies; and to toast 'the immortal memory of John of Gaunt'. When Celia Fiennes visited Hungerford she remarked that the town 'is famous for crayfish, there being a good river and great quantetys of that fish and large'. But Hungerford's role in history is not limited to fish and frolics, for it was here, while lodging at the Bear Inn, that Prince William of Orange, having landed near Torbay with a force of Anglo-Dutch troops, received the emissaries of his father-in-law, James II, whose throne he proposed to usurp. James had already sealed his own fate by trying to impose Roman Catholicism on a Protestant people. Macaulay set the scene as the Prince arrived: 'Late on Thursday, the sixth of December, he reached Hungerford. The little town was soon crowded with men of rank and note who came thither from opposite quarters. The Prince was escorted by a strong body of troops. The northern lords brought with them hundreds of irregular cavalry, whose accoutrements and horsemanship moved the mirth of men accustomed to the splendid aspect and exact movements of regular armies.' Two days later the King's representatives arrived. 'The Prince's bodyguard,' Macaulay continued, 'was drawn up to receive them with military respect.' There the courtesy ended, for, instead of obtaining a private audience with the Dutchman, the royalists 'were ushered into his bedchamber, where they found him surrounded by a crowd of noblemen and gentlemen ... the proposition which the Commissioners had been instructed to make was that the points in dispute should be referred to Parliament ...' It was indeed an agonizing reappraisal of a subject's allegiance and of the King's misrule. Many good men must have felt thankful when James fled the country, thereby allowing William to seize the throne. The Jacobites may have felt a shade less downcast when, in 1694, the first oil lamps appeared in London, having been placed along Kensington High Street specially to guide William of Orange to and from the Palace. In those years Kensington was a rural suburb, much frequented by footpads. Yet life goes on, King or no King. When, therefore, the noblemen and gentlemen departed, the townsfolk of Hungerford strolled as usual beside the Kennet, discussing the prospect of next year's harvest, the indiscipline of modern youth, the pains of age, the perils of matrimony, the price of ale, and the woman next door.

My journey began at the canal bridge across the lower end of the main street. Descending some stone steps, I found two waterside cottages—named Kennet and Avon—whose flowerbeds glowed with dahlias and hydrangeas. In lieu of a lawn, the cottages overlooked a grassy towing-path. On the far side of the canal stood a wharf that was built when the Industrial Revolutionaries created a network of inland waterways far surpassing the range of modern railways. This particular waterway was authorized by Parliament in 1794, its purpose being to link the Kennet at Newbury with the Avon at Bath. The first section, between Newbury and Hungerford, was opened in 1798 by 'a barge freighted with a wrought Portland stone staircase for J. Pearce Esq., of Chilton Lodge, a large quantity of deals, and nine cauldrons of sea coal, in all amounting to 40 tons'. The canal company must have been thankful when the first barge passed unmolested on her lawful occasions, because the opening of the Kennet Navigation from Reading to Newbury had met with violent opposition. Fearing that the new waterway would injure their trade, a mob of Reading townsfolk destroyed some of the workings. Five years later they drained some of the canal water. Encouraged by their Mayor, Recorder, and Aldermen, they then proceeded to smash a weir that was being constructed at Sheffield Lock. According to an old book, called *Kennet Country*, an eyewitness at 7 a.m. saw 'numbers of men with axes, large sticks and clubs on the road ...' Twelve hours later, the damage having been done, the witness saw 'great crowds of people returning back again to Reading, about 7 in the evening, dancing with music before them'. Half a century later, Britain contained so many canals that few places south of Durham were more than ten miles from a string of barges. Elderly townsfolk could remember Hungerford Lock when it was a busy port of call, but now the busyness had gone. Only a pair of swans passed by, like white and stately ships. Having overtaken the swans, I heard the splash of paddles, and turned to see a small barge in mid-stream, laden with volunteers outward bound to repair the banks. In short, Hungerford was the headquarters of a Trust that maintained the obsolete canal in a state of good repair.

Although the month was October, the green road looked dry and firm; the sky burned as blue as in August; and midges wove random patterns on the warmth. Once again, therefore, the sun had blessed my setting out, and a tideless canal answered the prayer which Edmund Spenser addressed to a tidal river:

Sweet Thames, run softly, till I end my Song.

Striding at four miles an hour, I thought I had left Hungerford behind, but after about a quarter of a mile I sighted the parish church, alone in a field beside the canal. It was neither an ancient nor a handsome church, having been built in 1815, at a time when men could still design beautiful homes, but had already lost the will and the skill to design beautiful churches. The priest, however, observed an old custom, for a notice in the porch said: 'People entering this church are reminded that by authority of the Bishop of Oxford the Holy Sacrament is reserved ...' To the men who built the Abbot's Way that notice would have seemed proper; to the men who built the Kennet and Avon Canal it would have seemed Popery.

Soon the roofs of Hungerford really did recede, and the path went its own way, accompanied by a silent railway from London to Penzance and by a loud road from London to Bath. Fortunately, the road soon turned north-east while the railway seemed congenial, like the prospect of meeting an acquaintance who neither calls too often nor stays too long. On, then, I went, through a series of slow arcs along a green road beside still waters under the lee of wooded hills in Berkshire, anciently called *Berrocscire*, the shire of *berroc silva* or 'wooded hills'. Miss Mitford described the Berkshire landscape as rather tame: 'so peaceful, so cheerful, so varied, so thoroughly English'. But Miss Mitford's *Our Village* was set at Five Mile Cross near Reading, whereas my own journey had almost reached the Wiltshire border, a region loftier than Reading. On the right, for example, rose the outriders from the Marlborough Downs, seemingly raised above their true height by a haze of autumnal sunshine.

After a couple of miles I heard a train. In the days of steam trains I would have stared enraptured, but now I did not trouble to glance round, because the train belched no smoke, showered no sparks, flashed no pistons. It did not even whistle. It was merely quicker, cleaner, and costlier than steam locomotion.

The passing train heightened the stillness of the lock near
the Kennet Valley Fisheries. Then a second train clattered
by, a sound and apparition that would have sent the Romans
reeling. The canal, however, they would have recognized
as a replica of their own handiwork in East Anglia. As with
roads, so with canals; Britain waited more than a thousand
years before she built as the Romans had done. The pio-
neers of our canals were businessmen seeking cheap transport for their wares; men like Josiah Wedgwood, who
financed the Trent and Mersey Canal. The chief purposes
of a canal were cited by a famous canal-builder, Thomas
Telford: '1st, For conveying the produce of Mines to the
Sea Shore. 2d, Conveying Food and Raw Materials to some
manufacturing Towns and Districts, and exporting the
Manufactured Goods. 3rd, Conveying Groceries and Merchant goods for the purposes of Agriculture; transporting
the produce of the District through which the Canal passes,
to the different Markets; and promoting Agricultural purposes generally.' Opposition to canals came chiefly from landowners and millers who feared that drainage would impair
their streams and watermeadows.

I had just got into my stride when the loud road reappeared, coming uncomfortably close while the canal curved
south-west towards Little Bedwyn. But the alarm was brief.
The road soon swerved out of sight and sound, due west
through Froxfield, there to harass the inmates of the Somerset Hospital, a glorious cluster of red brick, built in 1694 as
'Almshouses for 30 Poor Widows, founded and enlarged by
the right noble Sarah, Duchess of Somerset'. Froxfield's
Saxon name was *Forcansfeld*, the *feld* or 'open country' near
a *forsc* or 'frog stream'. The village stands a few hundred
yards inside the border of *Wiltunscir*, the shire whose capital
was Wilton.

At the next lock—either the fifth or the sixth since
Hungerford—a fisherman sat beside the water, pensive as
Rodin's *penseur*, yet cheerful withal, as though confirming
Sir Henry Wooton's avowal that angling was 'a rest to his

mind, a chearer of his spirits, a diverter of sadness, a calmer of unquiet thoughts, a moderator of passions, a procurer of contentedness ...' Simultaneously, as with one voice, the angler and I said: 'Lovely morning.' Then I strode on, pausing to pick blackberries and to admire the tapestry of yellow and scarlet and brown among woods beyond the water: Jugg's Wood, Stype Wood, Oak Wood, and Almshouse Copse (a perquisite of the Somerset Hospital). Another train passed, eighty-mile-an-houring to Q's Delectable Duchy, along a route that was conceived on 21 February 1833, when Isambard Kingdom Brunel scribbled in his diary a cryptic 'BR' or British Railway, soon to become the Great Western. Brunel had ridden this way, plotting a course through cornfields, over rivers, across marshes, under hills. Between Streatly and Hungerford he found the going very hard: 'Started at 6 a.m.,' said his diary, 'examined the ground in the neighbourhood of Wantage ... breakfasted at Streatly.' A day or two later he was 'Up at 5 a.m. .... ranged on the island east of Caversham. Breakfasted and mounted. Rode to meet Hughes ... found him in barley west of cottage. Rode to Basildon Farm ... tried in every way to find a line round instead of crossing the river ... found it impossible.' At remote inns he studied maps until dawn dimmed the candle, and it was time to ride out once more. 'Between ourselves,' he told a friend, 'it is harder work than I like. I am rarely at it much under twenty hours a day.' He was then only twenty-seven years old.

Brunel supervised every aspect of railway building and management. Having chosen a route, he designed the stations and the signal boxes and the bridges; and when the railway was at last running he complained to an entrepreneur who provided refreshments at Swindon Station: 'Dear Sir,' he wrote, 'I assure you Mr Player was wrong in supposing that I thought you purchased inferior coffee. I thought I said to him I was surprised you should buy such bad roasted corn. I did not believe you had any such thing as coffee in the place; I am certain I never tasted any. I have long since ceased to make complaints at Swindon. I avoid taking anything there when I can help it. Yours faithfully, I. K. Brunel.' Like his father—a Norman emigré—Brunel received a knighthood. He was, in fact, a giant among the Industrial Revolutionaries who were transforming not only the look of the land but also the lives of the people and the history of the world. Under their aegis, England became a pioneer of processes which diverted a large part of civilization from agriculture to industry, from fresh to stale air, from active to sedentary work. English agriculture—once the envy of Europe—so declined that in 1976 most of our food was imported.

What's in a name? The answer must include, 'A psychological response.' Berkshire, for example, evokes images of outer suburbia at Ascot and Maidenhead. But Wiltshire evokes images of deep country at Wilton and Stonehenge. Moreover, the county is wide as well as deep: 'Enclosed,' said William Camden, 'with Somersetshire on the West, Berkshire and Hampshire on the East; on the north with Gloucestershire; and on the south, with Dorsetshire, and a part of Hampshire.' Wiltshire, he added, 'is exceeding fertile, and plentiful of all things, yea, and for the varitie thereof, passing pleasant and delightsome.' Defoe discovered that Wiltshire was a seed-bed of history: 'The downs and plains in this part of England, being so open, and the subject so little subject to alteration, that there are more remains of antiquity to be seen upon them, than in any other places ... they tell me there are three hundred and fifty ancient encampments and fortifications to be seen in this one county.'

As on the derelict railway beside the Icknield Way, I paused to admire the workmanship of an earlier age, notably at Fore Bridge, whose bricks were of excellent quality, well laid to a simple yet graceful design. Mellowed by many weathers, their reddish tint merged with the October scene. The canal buildings and installations were the products of a pre-technical era, shaming our misuse of the word 'technology', which is a Greek compound, meaning 'craftsmanship'.

The speed and variety of mechanical inventions during the Industrial Revolution was without precedent. In 1733 Kay and Arkwright invented the flying shuttle; in 1759 James Brindley built what was virtually the first British canal since the Roman occupation; in 1764 Hargreaves invented the spinning jenny, and was followed by Crompton's 'mule' and Cartwright's power loom. Between 1796 and 1801 Trevithick designed a steam tramcar; then Davy invented the miner's safety lamp, and in 1821 George Stephenson became chief engineer of the Stockton and Darlington Railway. Weaving and spinning moved from cottages into mills. Between 1750 and 1830 the population of England more than doubled itself, rising from six to thirteen million. Food production was sacrificed on the altar of factories where women worked fourteen hours a day (their five-year-old daughters were not allowed to work more than twelve hours a day). The grimy snowball gathered mass and momentum, crushing crafts and customs and landscapes; building railways and roads and canals. The master-builders of those canals were a mixed bunch: James Brindley, a millwright; Thomas Telford, a stonemason; Benjamin Outram, a country gentleman; Thomas Smeaton, an attorney's son. The man who built the Kennet and Avon Canal was John Rennie, a Haddingtonshire odd-jobber, born in 1761. Self-taught, he designed machinery for the Albion Flour Mills in London. While still in his twenties he turned to canal-building and finally to harbour-building at Chatham, Sheerness, and Holyhead. In the years before nationalized transport made huge losses at the taxpayers' expense, competition forced the canals to keep their charges as low as possible, so that in 1863 a ton of iron was carried at the rate of one penny per mile. In 1838, at the peak of its prosperity, the Kennet and Avon Canal carried 341,878 tons of goods, nearly six times the tonnage carried by the Thames and Severn Canal. Indeed, the canal died of prosperity, because the Great Western Railway bought it and then allowed it to decay, thereby eliminating a competitor. Between 1845 and 1847 the railways bought and then neglected 948 miles of waterways, including the Kennet and Avon, the Thames and Severn, the Trent and Mersey, and the Shropshire Union. If railways could not buy a canal, they ruined it by under-cutting their own freight charges and then making up the deficit by delving into their passenger profits. On the Loughborough Navigation, for example, the rate per ton in 1836 was 2s 6d. A few years later the rate was forced down to 4d, and the company soon afterwards collapsed. Some of the other canals were more fortunate, like the one near my childhood home in north Buckinghamshire. This leisurely waterway carried many horse-hauled barges, led by a man or by a boy, and steered by a woman. Each barge was gaily painted and brilliantly polished. The spick-and-span cabin contained a black-leaded kitchen range, curtains, flowers, photographs, cushions ... all enhancing a floating home. Several locks kept a chandler's shop, where women bought food and other necessities. Sometimes an old dame in her waterside cottage taught the barge children to read and write while their mothers went shopping. In short, the bargefolk were a race apart, and proud to be so.

Immersed in those memories, I glanced over my shoulder, half-expecting to see a barge. But none appeared. The canal was empty. Yet what excitement must have heralded the men who built it; the surveyors, the engineers, the labourers. Here, surely, the story of Stane Street and Offa's Dyke was rewritten *à la mode*. Gazing from cottage windows, or leaning on their ploughs, countryfolk watched the deep trench creeping closer every day. Trees were felled, embankments were raised, piles were driven, pumps were installed, tunnels were dug. The Romans and the Saxons would have gaped at the engines and cranes that lightened the workmen's task. The course of navigation of a canal was dug by 'navigators', a name that appeared about the year 1780, and was abbreviated to 'navvies' in 1832. Some of the navvies were Irish; others were Fensmen—the fierce 'Fen Tigers'— accustomed to digging dykes; and all of them could become riotous like the navvies who in 1812 complained that they had been cheated by a local baker. Their riot ended as a bloody battle in which thirteen constables proved powerless until a troop of cavalry arrived to reinforce them. The Kennet and Avon Canal employed a doctor to tend the sick and injured workmen, some of whom formed their own insurance groups. Idleness was not unknown. One foreman reported that a certain Richard Jones was 'not at work at 2 o'clock P.M. nor had been in work all day. All his men Drinking except three men ...' Jones was promptly dismissed. In those days they ordered such things differently.

Very few regions in Britain, if any at all, can be described as free from man-made noise, since nowadays even Land's End and John o'Groat's are both close to an airport. At Fore Bridge, however, I was nearly eighty miles from London, so that I could not actually smell the place. The landscape, in fact, grew quieter than ever. The hills were higher, and the woods wider. At yet another bridge I halted again; and again no barge appeared. The only shipping was a brace of moorhens. Above the silence, I seemed to overhear a voice from the Icknield Way: 'Poetry is better than prose.' Following my own calling, therefore, I composed a brief history of the canal, chapter by chapter while I walked, beginning at the beginning:

> I walk where cottage housewives stared
> To see and hear the navvying crowd
> Who felled the fox's covert; bared
> The amber stubble; drained the shroud
> Of stagnant pond-scum; through the hill
> Tunnelled a fairway dark and eerie;
> Their shovels sharp, their curses shrill,
> Their faces brown, their muscles weary.

On the next sector I encountered a muddy patch, sheltered from sun and wind by overhanging branches. Had it not been for the volunteers, the path would have degenerated

into an overgrown swamp. The mud meanwhile showed footprints, and the footprints continued the history:

> I walk among the hidden grooves
> Where many feet and many hooves
> Once ventured; where the crews once hauled
> Laden barges, and loudly called
> A drowsy keeper to his lock
> At summer noons, or when the clock
> Chimed twilit teatime, and the snow
> Muffled a woman's voice below,
> Crooning her newborn son asleep,
> Snug in his cabin-cradle, deep
> Beneath the dripping gates, beneath
> The frozen hills beyond the heath.

The railway still accompanied the waterway, but only two
or three trains had passed since I left Hungerford. The rest
was sunlight, robins, rooks, crows, sheep, and one faraway
tractor droning home to dinner. The next bridge (I had long
since lost count of them) carried a lane that sent a branch
beside the left bank, sandwiching the waterway between the
railway and the byway. But still no train appeared; no pedestrian, no motorist, no one at all. Even the fish had ceased to
rise. All things indulged in an October siesta, or so it seemed,
until I noticed a battered trilby hat, just visible above the
hedge on my left. It belonged to an aged man who was
cycling more slowly than I thought possible; the pedals
scarcely turning, yet the wheels forever moving. Once more
I said: 'Lovely morning.' With the poise of a professional
acrobat, the veteran glanced over the hedge. 'It is an' all,' he
agreed, adding: 'I'm in no 'urry.'

'Nor,' I assured him, 'am I.'

The man then set his left leg at right angles to the lane,
after which he leaned against the bank, and slowly—for he
was indeed in no hurry—dismounted. To myself I said: 'As
along the Icknield Way and the Scottish drove road, Methu-
selah is about praise the past and thereby uncover it.'

'I suppose,' the man said, 'you want to know about the

canal. Well, I'll tell you. It used to be full, and now it's empty.'

I waited for him to continue, but he merely turned his machine round, and slowly went back by the way he had slowly come. More than that I cannot say, because I do not know.

Unlike the builders of Stane Street, John Rennie aimed at levelness, not at directness, because every cutting and every lock added to the cost. Therefore the canal twisted, like water seeking its own level. At this point, however, the by-way and the railway and the waterway were following a fairly straight course, past yet another bridge and yet another lock, and after that a red-brick cottage, gay-gardened, nappy-clothes-lined, but no longer a part of the canal. Edward Thomas had witnessed a similar dereliction:

> Only the idle foam
> Of water falling
> Ceaselessly calling,
> Where once had been a work-place and a home.

Now I began to look for an old friend, Little Bedwyn, whose gardens at the appropriate season illustrate the hamlet's name, a dialect word, *bedwind*, meaning 'clematis'. Presently I sighted the church tower among trees on the far side of the water. Bisected by the railway and the canal, Little Bedwyn is beautiful, unpretentious, sequestered. Its southern and higher half contains two handsome houses, several cottages, and the Harrow Inn, a name well suiting thirsty men who, having ploughed the fields, scatter the seed and then return to harvest it. The larger of the two houses is a chequer-brick Georgian mansion, shielded by high walls that were built by a generation for whom privacy was not a luxury but a necessity. The second house—whitewashed and less stately—stands within a few yards of the canal, where the green road becomes a wide lawn alongside an idle lock. The only eyesore is a modern concrete bridge joining both parts of the hamlet. From that bridge you look down on a row of cottages, including one which may be the smallest Post Office in Britain. The rest of Little Bedwyn—perhaps a dozen cottages—lies along a cul-de-sac facing the canal. At the far end of the cul-de-sac stands the church, a stone-and-flint amalgam of Norman arcades, Early English tower, and Perpendicular nave. On my way to the church I rested briefly at a timber seat that was set there in 1971 by a local benefactress, Mrs E. B. Gauntlett. While cattle grazed in the meadow, and sunlight dimpled the water beyond them, I felt some sympathy with Cobbett's notion of an ideal place in which to live. His own choice, he said, had been 'always very much divided between the woods of Sussex and the downs of Wiltshire. I should not like to be compelled to decide : but if I were compelled, I do believe that I should fix on some vale in Wiltshire.'

Little Bedwyn is indeed an old friend of mine. I am always glad to reach it, and always sorry to leave it. However, the sun shone, the robins sang, and I continued in a more or less direct course south-west to Great Bedwyn. The lane thither had switched from the left to the right of the canal, under the lee of Chisbury Camp, the hilltop site of a Celtic earthwork, covering fifteen acres. Many years earlier I had seen the small Georgian manor house within the camp, and a thatched chapel, almost in ruins, dedicated to St Martin.

At the next bend a stationary tractor peered over the hedge. It was there that I lay down in the sun while ducks ruffled the water within a yard of my head, and crows pecked the furrows within a yard of my feet. The absence of any fellow-travellers led me to forget that I had a destination. I appeared to be exploring a country where Time itself lay down in the sun. Eventually I did reach Great Bedwyn railway station, close to the canal. It is a dreary station, outmoded by motors, ignored by all save a few trains, and nationalized into nonentity. But when I first knew it the station was cluttered with crates, churns, passengers, and a grey-haired railwayman who did everything except drive the trains. And how proud they all were of being Great Western!

'Run to time?' they used to say. 'Don't talk daft. 'Tis Time runs to us when it wants to know how long afore the next train's due.'

Great Bedwyn village cannot be compared with its little namesake, for although the old houses are comely, the main street is marred by a secondhand car mart (who, I wondered, went thither on such business?). In the brick-and-stone church beside the canal lies Sir John Seymour, father of the Jane Seymour who married Henry VIII a few days after Anne Boleyn's execution. Doctors remember Thomas Willis FRS (born at Great Bedwyn in 1621), who studied medicine at Oxford before he became professor of natural philosophy. Willis specialized in the treatment of diabetes and in the topography of the brain, part of which is still called Willis's Circle. He was buried in Westminster Abbey.

The canal now approached Savernake Forest, formerly *Safernoc*, a Celtic river-name comparable with Severn, and probably referring to the River Bedwind. By crossing some fields I soon reached the first glade. The whole Forest shone. Every tree looked as if it had been polished from topmost twig to rooted bole. When Celia Fiennes rode through the Forest in 1703 she met some of its oldest inhabitants: 'Its 8 miles to Hungerford over Savernack Forest, where is much deer ...' In 1976 the Forest covered five thousand acres, and was leased from the Crown at a peppercorn rent by the Marquess of Ailesbury, who allowed the public to wander at will, subject only to the basic courtesies of *meum et tuum*. Earlier marquesses gave the Forest a Frenchified appearance by building straight avenues and tall monuments, notably the Grand Avenue (four miles long) and the Ailesbury Column (commemorating George III's recovery from a period of psychosis). In the depths of the Forest stands Tottenham House, a mansion that was built for the Ailesburys during the early years of the nineteenth century, but in 1976 was occupied by a school.

Savernake Forest is a sequence of sylvan solitudes, interspersed with a few fields and lanes. On those solitudes

October cast its customary spell, ever-old yet always new. Looking up at the trees and at the sky between them I felt as though I were an airman, peering down on a maze of blue lakes in a land of bronze furrows, with here a scarlet streak and there a yellow. Through the still air a leaf fluttered down, then another and a third and somewhere far off a fourth; all swaying silently, gracefully, and over a wide area, rather like the random raindrops that precede a storm. Falling, they caught the sun, and were as jewels. It was sad, though, to see several elm trees either dead or dying, victims of a disease that had killed millions of such trees during the past decade. In simple terms, Dutch elm disease is a cancerous growth, caused and carried by insects. It reached England during the 1920s, in a relatively mild and localized form. If a diseased elm is felled and burned, its neighbours may escape untouched, but once the contagion has spread widely, the chances of halting it are at present slight. Fortunately, the elms in Savernake Forest were greatly outnumbered by other species, notably beech and British oak, the *Quercus robur* which eighteenth-century admirals used to sow as acorns on their estates, hoping that the trees would one day reinforce Britain's shield of timber ships.

From the forest's fiery solitude I returned to the canal; and still no one appeared. In the mountains, of course, a traveller may expect to walk alone, but when the absence of humanity is accompanied by a road and a railway and a canal, the effect becomes eerie.

At Crofton pumping station I reached the canal's highest point, four hundred feet above the River Kennet. The history of the pumping station can be summarized thus: faced by a two-mile climb, and lacking enough water, Rennie proposed to bring a supply from a lake that lay a mile to the east of the canal, and at a lower level. He therefore consulted one of his previous employers, Boulton and Watt of Birmingham, who designed two steam-driven pumps, each able to raise eleven tons of water per minute. The tall-chimneyed engine-house was built of brick, to a simple yet agreeable pattern, conspicuously different from modern power-houses. The pumps which Rennie installed are said to be the oldest working beam engines in the world. That they were working regularly until 1958 is a tribute to the Georgian engineers. In 1968 the engines and engine-house were bought and renovated by the Kennet and Avon Canal Trust, to whom our industrial archaeologists are indebted.

A ribbon of smoke rose from the chimney as I approached. Leaving the canal, I went to investigate, and at last met another human being, who informed me that this w: one of six weekends each year when the pumps are set to work for the entertainment of all whom they may concern. Feeling no concern for any kind of machinery I did not enter the engine-house, but chose rather to visit the hamlet of Wilton, on the far side of the canal. There I found *inter alia* a duck pond, some thatched cottages, a dissenting chapel, and a memorial to John Wesley at Orchard House, formerly Bank House, whose deeds require (or used to require) the owner neither to remove nor allow to be removed the Wesley Stone marking the place where the evangelist preached an open-air sermon. The clause in the lease of Bank House reminded me of the inscription on a silver cup at Pembroke College, Cambridge, cursing anyone who removed the cup: *Qui alienaverit anathema sit.*

Back at Crofton, I found that my informant had vanished. The solitude then seemed more than ever uncanny because Crofton contained a railway, a pumping station, several locks, several lanes, and a second or feeder canal; yet of man there was no sign nor sound until someone whistled his dog at Freewarren Farm. Beyond Crofton the canal altered course, bearing gradually south-west towards Martinsell Hill, nearly a thousand feet up. Was it from there that Richard Jefferies sighted the Marlborough Downs, and heard their silence? 'The long, long slopes,' he wrote, 'the endless ridges, the gaps between, hazy and indistinct, are absolutely without noise.' Surely it was in weather such as this that he wrote the next sentence: 'In the sunny autumn day the peace of the sky overhead is reflected into the silent earth.' Only one thing was missing ... the barges and their crew, voyaging through a pageant that varied from hour to hour, from lock to lock, from season to season.

At a place called Stibb Green the canal reached the meridian of its northern arc, thereafter dropping south-west, only a mile or so from Burbage, a hotch-potch of old houses shining like good deeds in a bungaloid world. What a pity, I thought, that our forefathers held such a low opinion of hygiene, and that our contemporary architects positively dislike beauty. In Burbage stood Wolf Hall, incorporating part of the birthplace of Queen Jane, Henry VIII's third wife. Burbage men (or such of them as still care for such things) will tell you that the King spent four days at Wolf Hall, courting its daughter; that he felt inhibited by the presence of his potential in-laws; and that the family therefore moved to an adjacent barn. If the story is true, the King must have gone a-wooing while he was still married. According to Lord Herbert of Cherbury, 'the King proceeded to his intended marriage ... as some say, the day following Queen Anne's death, others till three days after ...' Anne Boleyn having been executed for treason, the widower did not think it 'fit to mourn long, or too much, for one the law had declar'd criminal ...' Lord Herbert himself gave a good account of the lady from Burbage: 'This Queen certainly deserved all the favour done her, as being reputed the discreetest, fairest, and humblest of the King's wives ...' Although the new Queen presented the King with what both he and his subjects most desired, a legitimate male heir, the rejoicing was tinged with sadness: 'two days after her delivery [she] died; and was buried in the quire at Windsor; whose loss much affected the King ... insomuch notwithstanding some good offers made him, he continued a widower for more than two years ...' So anxious was the father to establish the son, that the week-old infant was created Prince of Wales, Duke of Cornwall, and Earl of Cornwall.

Somewhere a distant clock chimed noon, and I guessed that it came from my next port of call, Wooton or 'the town in the woods', an attractive village straddling the canal with brick, timbered, and thatched cottages. The dial of the church clock, instead of being numbered, told the time by means of twelve letters which spelt *Glory Be To God*. At Wooton I expected to meet several human beings. Perhaps because it was lunchtime, I met none. After some searching, however, I found a little girl sunning herself under a chestnut tree. In the course of our conversation she told me that the church clock commemorated the coronation of King George V; that its maker was Jack Spratt; and that its materials were old bedsteads and old perambulators. The child evidently shared Dr Johnson's belief that it is better to know than not to know something, no matter how trivial the something may be. For my part, I told her that at Buckland-in-the-Moor in Devonshire the clock spells *My Dear Mother*. And with that we said good-bye, pleased to have met each other.

Refreshed and informed, I continued westwards into sunshine, admiring the sweep of the Marlborough Downs, which in William Cobbett's day were so barren that he lodged one of his explosive complaints: 'I looked ... over the flat towards Marlborough, and there I saw ... rascally heaths. So that this villainous tract extends from East to West, with more or less exceptions, from Hounslow to Hungerford.' Some of Cobbett's imprecations must be swallowed *cum grano*, but on this occasion his indignation was shared by Thomas Davis of Longleat, bailiff to the Marquess of Bath. In 1794 Davis informed the Board of Agriculture: 'There is on Marlborough downs a tract of some hundred acres, called "Albourn Chace", which may truly be called "waste land", and, in its present situation, a blot on the country ...' Cobbett, an eloquent peasant-farmer, could not see the point of buying from foreigners the food which we ought to produce for ourselves. When he reached the Kennet and Avon Canal he vented his anger thereon: 'We crossed a canal at a place where there is a wharf and a coal-yard, and close by these a gentleman's house, with coach-house, stables, walled-in garden ... when, upon further inquiry ... I found that it was the villa of the chief manager; could not help congratulating the proprietors of this aquatic concern; for, although I did not ask the name of the canal, I could readily suppose, that the profits must be prodigious.' But we ought not to misinterpret Cobbett's contentiousness. Like a good Englishman, he spoke out when he felt that he must; and especially did he speak out against what he felt to be evil in his own day. But—like a truly amateur boxer—he never hit harder than the limit set by sportsmanship, which is leavened with courtesy and humanity.

By this time the green road had brought me close to the Vale of Pewsey, where gravel and chalk caused much trouble when Rennie tried to build a watertight course for his canal. The hills, too, proved formidable. In fact, they compelled him to set no fewer than twenty-nine locks along the fifteen miles between Wootton Rivers and Devizes, some only a boat's-length apart, and in a dead straight line. But, as we have noted, the fruits of his skill were destroyed prematurely. Within three years—from 1844 to 1847—nearly a thousand miles of canals were bought by railway companies which then allowed them to decay. In 1830 Britain contained about three thousand miles of navigable canals; in 1976, only a few hundred miles.

My admiration of Rennie's achievement reached its peak when I reached the Savernake Summit Tunnel, more than five hundred yards long. An inscription on the eastern entrance stated that the tunnel was named Bruce, in recognition of encouragement received from Thomas Bruce, Earl of Ailesbury, and from his son, Charles. As a child I had often watched barges emerging from tunnels, propelled by men who lay on the cabin roof while their legs walked on the tunnel roof. Meantime, I was not sorry to pass from dank gloom back again into shimmering sunshine. The Marlborough Downs looked more majestic than ever; the

Savernake Forest, more fiery; and up from the stubble sprang a lark, blithe as a black minim on a blue score.

At the penultimate bridge before Pewsey a horse trotted down to the towing-path. He was a good-looking creature, but very broad in the beam, no doubt for want of a day's hunting. Not having any sugar to offer, I placed a few flakes of tobacco in the palm of my hand, knowing that some animals like to chew the cud. This animal, however, was a non-smoker. He sniffed and then trotted away. But back he came, still at the trot, as though seeking companionship. While patting his mane, and agreeing that these were indeed lonely surroundings, I was confounded by the throb of a distant boat. Hurrying to the next bridge (it was called Pains), I saw a blue and scarlet paddleboat, rippling the water at four knots while her helmsman stared ahead, vigilant as Cortes scanning the horizon for a landfall. When the boat drew abeam I called the day's third greeting: 'Lovely afternoon.'

'Lovely,' the helmsman nodded.

'Paddles, I see.'

'Screws can get fouled in the weeds.'

'Going far?'

'Pains. Laying her up for the winter.'

'Are there many boats on this canal?'

'Depends what you mean by many.' He glanced astern. 'At Pewsey you'll find a dozen or so.'

Such is an old sailor's love of ships—even of freshwater paddleboats—that I stared after the pleasure craft as a Tudor merchant might have watched his vessel sail westward to the world's end and to whatever fate awaited her ... pirates, perhaps, or shipwreck, or a safe return with silk and silver and spice. The brief encounter with the paddleboat reminded me that a few steam-driven barges had first appeared on the canal in 1852, when the company experimented with a variable pitch propeller.

The next quarter-mile led straight to Pewsey Wharf, which really was a wharf, stone-built for loading and unloading barges; with offices and warehouses in fair condition, and a slipway for pleasure craft moored alongside. On the opposite bank, facing the Pewsey road, stood an inn, the French Horn, where I met the day's second veteran, very knowledgeable about bargefolk. 'Most of 'em were steady chaps,' he told me, 'except when they'd had a few pints. Then they'd out-cuss the Bible itself. You never heard such a trans-migration o' language.'

'What about the men who actually built the canal?' I asked.

'The navvies? Now they really were a tough bunch. Es-pecially the Irish. My old Dad knew about the navigators. Heard it from his grandpa, no doubt. As soon as those navvies appeared, the rabbits disappeared. Ah, and the chicken popu-lation didn't exactly multiply. Dad used to say the Irish were friendly in an unfriendly way. The rector found two of 'em fighting one day. Fair bruised and bloody they were. But when he tried to stop 'em they joined forces and knocked him down.'

'Another beer?' I suggested.

'Well, I never say No to any gent as wishes me to say Yes.'

My reward was on earth, and it took the form of a final reminiscence. 'The bargemen didn't like it when the canal began to fail. Old Zebedee, for instance. A real Primitive Baptist was Zeb. Strict as Zion itself. "Mark my words," he used to say, "when the barges have gone, this sinful genera-tion shall suffer a gnashing and wailing of teeth." And he wasn't far wrong, was he? I see in this morning's paper, beer's going up again.'

Leaving the taproom to its immemorial talk, I went out into the sunshine. My journey was now nearing its end; but before reaching it, I strolled into the little town of Pewsey, several of whose shops are thatched, and many of the houses mellow, notably the old Georgian rectory, which became a local council office. A statue of King Alfred bestrides the main street, recalling the fact that he once held the manor of Pewsey. Alfred was born in the neighbouring county of

Berkshire, where his father held the royal manor of Wantage. The parish church contains Norman arcades and a reredos that was carved by Canon Pleydell-Bouverie, rector from 1880 until 1910. The altar rail—presented by the third Earl Nelson—is a piece of mahogany from a Spanish warship, the *San Josef*, wherefrom hangs the following tale: in 1797 an English Fleet, numbering only fifteen ships of the line, engaged a Spanish Fleet, numbering twenty-seven ships of the line as well as ten frigates and a brig. Among the English ships was HMS *Captain*, commanded by Commodore Horatio Nelson, who, after a daring manoeuvre, led a boarding party that captured the *San Nicholas* and the *San Josef*, whose Flag-Captain surrendered his sword. 'On the quarter-deck of a Spanish first-rate,' wrote Nelson, 'extravagant as the story may seem, I received the swords of the vanquished Spaniards which, as I received them, I gave to William Fearney, one of the bargemen, who put them, with the greatest *sang-froid*, under his arm.' Nelson's father, a Norfolk parson, heard the news while staying in Somerset, and at once wrote to congratulate his son: 'The name and services of Nelson,' he declared, 'have sounded throughout the city of Bath, from the common ballad singer to the public theatre.' Two weeks before the battle—though not in time for the news to reach him—Nelson was promoted Rear-Admiral of the Blue. After the battle, he received a knighthood.

The afternoon was still warm and bright when I returned to the Wharf. Hitherto the green road had traversed a wide landscape, with a lane and a railway nearby, but at Pewsey it entered a wooded and secretive sector, comparable with parts of the Thames above Oxford, where trees form an avenue above the water. At a first glance the atmosphere appeared pellucid, but a second glance showed that everything was touched with sunshine which, when it filtered among the branches, resembled pillars of golden haze. Some of the trees leaned so far across the canal that they created a bower of blue sky and burnished leaves. One of those leaves floated from its twig to its grave, where it lay like a piece of amber. Then a silver-snouted fish plopped up, as if to admire the ripples which it had caused; and whenever a robin sang, it seemed to be saying: 'Listen to the silence.' In that silence I continued my brief history of the canal:

> I walk through sparkling leaves that twine
> While robins sing, and fishes shine,
> And rabbits bask, and cattle browse
> Beside a path that many trod,
> Though now as quiet as Ichabod.

Similar sentiments were expressed, rather more precisely, by the twelve-volume report of a Royal Commission in 1909: 'On a few waterways traffic has been maintained ... on other waterways it has declined, on some it has virtually disappeared.' The Commission compiled a list of major canals which seemed worth keeping and improving. In 1958 the Bowes Committee recommended that 1,315 miles of waterways be retained. In 1962 the waterways were placed under the control of the British Waterways Board. Many canals are now used by pleasure boats, but it is unlikely that the commercial traffic will become as heavy as it was during the early nineteenth century.

Less than a mile beyond Pewsey Wharf a lane crossed the canal via Bristow Bridge, another graceful example of Georgian craftsmanship, mellow as the month itself. But instead of proceeding under the bridge, the towing-path disappeared; and although I climbed onto the lane and thence down to the water, I still could not find the vanished path. Only then did it occur to me that the path had switched to the opposite bank. So, I climbed back, crossed the bridge, and found the path. Musing in a brown-and-blue study, I invited myself to name the canal that crosses the most beautiful scenery in Britain. My verdict was a dead-heat between the Caledonian Canal through the Scottish Highlands, and the Shropshire Canal between Hurleston and Llangollen, offering views of the Pennines and the Welsh peaks. Second

place went to the Kennet and Avon Canal between Savernake Tunnel and the Avon Valley beyond Devizes.

In Lower Bristow Copse the branches almost brushed the
water. I was walking slowly now, as through a cathedral,
hushed by the stillness, and so dazzled by the tinted haze that
I scarcely noticed a gap in the hedge on my right. Vaguely
aware of a distant roof, I returned to the gap, which revealed Stowell Park, a neo-classical mansion, built in 1813.
The park adjoined the towing-path, and was studded with
trees, some of them palisaded against livestock. After a few
more yards I caught sight of a 1940 pillbox hidden among
bushes, only a few feet to right of the path. Clambering
over some barbed wire, I entered the war memorial. Its door-
less porch was shielded from within by a concrete wall. The
floor was paved with more than thirty autumns. The walls
were pierced by slits commanding a view of the canal. En-
cased in concrete, I thought of the men who had sweated
there on a summer afternoon, or shivered through a winter
night: farmfolk, foresters, postmen, gamekeepers, doctors,
lawyers, shop assistants, road-menders, farriers, vets,
butchers, bakers, old-age pensioners, and (if they then existed) candlestick-makers. To many people nowadays the
Home Guard is a joke, and the war against Hitler an archaic
example of sabre-rattling. Well, such people are still free to
think such things, because we, the archaics, drove back the
aggressor.

Then an incident occurred, trivial yet symbolic. Peering
through one of the slits, I sighted two youths in a canoe,
their paddles glinting as they caught the sun, each stroke
scattering a rainbow of spray. In larger craft the Vikings had
rowed up-river from the sea, to spread death and destruction
far inland, watched by fearful Celts and Saxons hiding in the
woods. When the canoe had passed, I stepped out of the war
memorial, and into the sunshine, over the lives of those who
died defending Britain:

> At the going down of the sun and in the morning
> We will remember them.

Now at last the trees on the left bank gave way to open fields, fringed by a few poplars. On the right, beyond Stowell Park, downland surged to the sky. Presently I passed under a high metal bridge, with a single wooden plank for passage. Next, a lane joined in from East Stowell, coming close to the canal, at which point stood a cottage whose overhanging thatch formed a loggia supported by three-pronged timbers. From the cottage I could now see my journey's end at Wilcot Bridge, less than half a mile away. On the Scottish drove road, you remember, my journey was crowned by a pleasant surprise when sheep and horsemen and dogs appeared, bringing new life to an old setting. No such climax occurred on the Kennet and Avon Canal. I was lucky to have met one canoe and one paddleboat, for the cruising season had ended, and the afternoon would soon follow suit. Lacking a tangible climax, I created one by staring westward into the sunlight and then screwing up my eyes until I saw only an impression of bright sky and shining water. Then I superimposed another impression by fancying that I heard the thud of a horse's hooves on a green road, and the swish of a bow-wave through a blue fairway. The details of the illusion scarcely mattered, and were in any event blurred by the haze. It was enough to be aware of the plodding horse, led by a barefoot urchin who sucked a straw. As the apparition drew nearer I blinked at the barge's brightwork gleaming in the sun. The cargo gleamed, too—as coal does gleam—heaped like an ebony Alp from the for'ard samson post to the cabin roof aft. In the deep cockpit a swarthy man held the tiller under his left arm while he steered by bending from the waist upward. He wore the kind of cloth cap that might have been seen at any time between the Battle of Inkerman and the rise of Mussolini. The smoke from his clay pipe drifted parallel with a larger plume from the stovepipe chimney. As the barge draw alongside I fancied I saw her name, *Savernake Sally*, painted bright red with pale blue scrolls. I felt certain I saw a woman at the cabin door, holding a child in her arms. She wore a white apron over a black silk dress. Like her husband, she was bronzed by the inland elements. It was not until the barge had passed by that I noticed a mongrel dog and a ginger cat sunbathing in coiled rope above the tiller. A fantasy? Yes indeed; yet a true replica of the reality which as a child I had seen in north Buckinghamshire. The moral, if there was one, resembled the sermon on the Icknield Way, where railways that had been superseded by canals were themselves overtaken by motorways. While the illusion lasted, I concluded my brief history :

> I walk where patient horses trod;
> Where farriers at their anvil shod
> Immense and shaggy Shires; where inns
> Sustained a multitude of sins
> And waterside compassion; where
> The bargemen set a midnight snare,
> And, as the sun rose, took good care
> That dawn should jug the stolen hare.
> I walk within a vanished world,
> Its barges beached, its ensigns furled,
> And all its skills and customs gone
> To an amphibious Avalon.

When I opened my eyes again, the sun was sinking behind the poplars on the far side of the water. While it still shone, I sat down in the grass, resolved to drain the last drop of drowsiness, for in two hours' time the green road would be dark and damp. Slowly yet perceptibly the golden haze dispersed. Leaves lost their lustre. The canal was rinsed of its blueness. Cold crept down from the sky and up from the water. Then I realized that I had chosen to rest in a shady patch.

By walking on I regained the sunshine, and within a few minutes reached the end of my journey, Wilcot Bridge, another pleasant structure, which carried a quiet country lane. Beside it stood some old thatched cottages and several modern bungalows. Both types of house have their merits and defects, and both were fairly assessed by W. H. Hudson, who preferred the old : 'Undoubtedly,' he agreed, 'they are darker inside, and not so convenient to live in as the modern, box-shaped, red-bricked, slate-roofed cottages, which have spread a wave of ugliness over the country ...' The new houses, Hudson continued, clash with their surroundings, but the old ones 'are weathered and coloured by sun and wind and rain and many lowly vegetable forms in harmony with nature'. Hudson then summed it up by saying that the old cottages are 'related to the trees amid which they stand, and to the sky and clouds over all ... And most delightful feature, they stand among, and are wrapped in, flowers.'

With that benediction I took leave of a green road which had carried me into several centuries, though the journey itself lasted no longer than a sunny autumn day.

The Sugarloaf Mountain

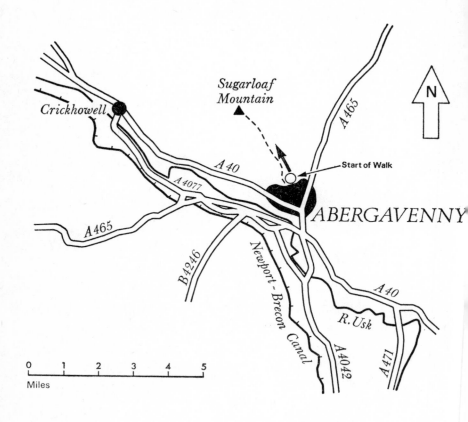

8 The Sugarloaf Mountain

IN so far as the journey was scarcely two miles long, and took place in Monmouthshire, some people would describe it as an English stroll. But I call it a Welsh climb, and shall presently justify the name. That the journey occurred at all was due chiefly to the weather, which began by confounding the forecast. It snowed, for one thing; for another, it blew. Seldom can a British sky have been so black, a British wind so bleak. At bedtime, therefore, I did not bother to hear the weather forecast. It had already misled me into travelling nearly two hundred miles. So ended my hope that February would grant a sunlit winterscape.

Next morning, however, I woke to a sky that seemed to have sailed from the Aegean overnight. The slush had gone, the air was mild, the mountains wore a sheen of snow. Having come so far, and being reluctant to give up without a struggle, I decided to compromise by venturing along a green road that was much shorter and slightly less weather-beaten than my first choice. So, in bright sunshine, I set out from Abergavenny, alias *Aber Gefenni* or 'mouth of the River Gefenni', in the county of Monmouth alias *Aber Mynwy* or 'mouth of the River Monow'. Set on the site of a Roman town, Abergavenny is steep, ancient, and surrounded by mountains. It contains a ruined castle that has belonged to the Neville family since the reign of Henry VII; also the remains of a priory that was razed by a very Welsh man, Owain Glyndwr.

On the northern edge of the town I stopped to consult three men who, by speaking Welsh, posed a question: is Monmouthshire Welsh or is it English? The map, though mute, gives a loud answer: Bettws-Newydd, Llangottockvibon-Avel, Pen Gloch y pibwr, Tal-cfyn, Pen Cerig calch, Llanfihangel-Crucorney: no Saxon there, no Angle, no Viking, no Norman. It is true, of course, that the sixteenth-century Acts of Union created the region as a new county, but nowhere did those Acts state that the county was henceforth to be English; on the contrary, Monmouth shared a common status with every other Welsh county. The poet Islwyn claimed that, by whatever name, Monmouthshire *is* Welsh:

> Gwyllt Walia, ydwyt tithau, Mynwy gu!
> Dy enw'n unig a newidiaist ti.

Moreover, Shakespeare's Captain Fluellen, a Monmouthshire man, reminded Henry V: 'I am Welsh, you know, good countryman.' The King assented, having himself been born in Monmouthshire. But the matter can be settled by something less vague than hearsay or personal bias. Thus, Monmouthshire lies within the Welsh diocese of Monmouth; a Welsh Board supervises the county's State schools; Welsh is taught in the grammar schools (or was, until class warfare destroyed those ancient academies of the common people); gas and electricity come respectively from the South Wales Gas Board and the South Wales Electricity Board; the county has a Welsh newspaper, the *South Wales Argus*; Monmouthshire men are eligible to play for the Welsh Rugby XV; and in 1956 the Home Office stated: 'In Whitehall terminology, Wales includes Monmouthshire.' By the end of the eighteenth century, however, Monmouthshire had lost much of its Welshness, at any rate in the opinion of Englishmen. Defoe, for example, implied that the county was *not* Welsh. Having reached Monmouth, he wrote: 'I am now at the utmost extent of England west ...'

Meanwhile, the Welsh-speaking trio whom I consulted might have passed as Spaniards, and were evidently of Celtic stock, like the village butcher near the Icknield Way. They told me that they had come down from Cardiganshire, where Welsh is still the fireside talk. 'Yes,' they added, in answer to my question, 'the mountain road will be walkable. There is snow on the top, mind, but not deep. You have chosen a good day. More like spring, surely?' Then they pointed north, along the Brecon road. 'You will see a sign on the left. Far?' They smiled. 'You will be there before you have changed gear.'

The sign was not quite so near as that, but I soon reached it, a National Trust sign pointing to a steep and narrow lane among trees and a few cottages and farms, each perched on its own rung of the mountain. The lane ended at a car park which in spring and summer would have been crammed, but was now as empty as an open-air theatre in December. On a ridge above the car park, I saw the green road toiling up from Abergavenny and thence to the domelike summit of the Sugarloaf Mountain, less than two miles away. In 1936 the mountain was given to the National Trust by the first and second Viscountesses Rhondda, as a memorial to David Alfred Thomas, first Viscount Rhondda, one of seventeen children of a grocer in Merthyr Tydfil. Business must have been brisk, because the grocer's boy went to Clifton and Cambridge. Father and son then turned to the coal mining trade, and grew richer still. During the First World War the son served as Food Controller, for which his slippery fellow-countryman, Lloyd George, gave him a peerage. Unlike some of Lloyd George's creations, this one was merited.

Since the Sugarloaf Mountain resembles an enormous green carpet, it may sound strange to speak of a green road thereon; but that is one of the virtues of such roads, for they are supererogations of greenness, recognizable because footsteps and hoofmarks have smoothed their surface. The prospect ahead was of bleak and high fertility. The bleakness lay on the summit; the fertility lay all around and far below. How old was the road itself? Some people believed that it had been created by the National Trust; others, that it was a Celtic track, leading to a shrine or perhaps a look-out post on the summit; others, again, said that it was a local drove road, or at any rate a road for sheep grazing on the mountain. One thing was certain; in summer the road carried thousands of visitors and hundreds of sheep. On this day there were neither sheep nor visitors.

Like George Borrow, the poet Twym o'r Nant wrote unkindly of the drovers:

> The old drover sleeps, his term completed;
> Throughout his wasted life he cheated.

Other drovers were more highly esteemed, like David Lloyd, who in the eighteenth century served Sir Watkin Williams-Wynn for nearly fifty years, and was entrusted with several thousand pounds sterling to pay London debts. Some of the Welsh drovers acted as government messengers, and a few founded their own bank, notably *Banc y Ddafa Ddu* (The Black Sheep Bank) at Aberystwyth, and *Banc yr Eidion* (The Black Ox Bank) at Llandovery. One drover, Thomas Williams of Llanfachreth, opened a book shop and a printing press. Another, Daffyd Jones of Caio, translated Isaac Watts's hymns into Welsh. Among the subscribers to Dr Johnson's *Plan of a Dictionary of the English Language* were four Welsh drovers: Thomas Roberts of Lyn Cwm, John Thomas of Bala, Hugh Parry of Penmorfe, and Thomas Jones of Ty Isaf. Such men received three shillings a day during each drove, plus six shillings on reaching their destination; to which was added whatever money they had earned by selling milk from their cows en route. Drovers preferred green roads to metalled, not least because the latter imposed turnpike dues. At the beginning of the nineteenth century 30,000 cattle were driven from South Wales every year. Local trade, too, was prosperous, with 3,000 cattle travelling from the Lleyn Peninsula to North Wales. Droving begets a great thirst, which is one reason why the Drovers Arms have not yet disappeared from inn signs. Even the livestock received a form of assistance, as, for example, at Painscastle—no great distance from the Sugarloaf—where cattle and ducks and geese received 'shoes' to help them on their journey to London via Hereford.

My own shoes, meanwhile, crunched through patches of snow which created a skewbald appearance as the green road climbed gently to a sharp bend and the final lap to the summit. For about half a mile the going was easy, but when I reached the bend, the real ascent began. More than once I sighted a lump of snow that might have been either a stoat or a mountain hare, both of which camouflage themselves in a white and wintry coat. I noticed, too, some signs of erosion near the summit, where several boulders were scattered. Erosion at such an altitude is inevitable because extremes of temperature cause the rocks to crack. The cracks then collect water; the water freezes; the ice widens the cracks; and the rain washes away any debris that has accumulated in the cracks. This process of leaching reduces the amount of vegetation that will grow on a mountain. Many of the rocks between the Sugarloaf and the Herefordshire hills are Old Red Sandstone, which gives the soil a pinkish glow. The study of rocks is a comparatively modern science. Medieval men were more concerned with alchemy and the search for gold, while Renaissance men preferred astronomy, chemistry, physics, and optics. In 1697 Edmund Halley conducted scientific experiments on Snowdon, but it was not until 1815 that William Smith, the so-called Father of English Geology, produced the first geological map of England and Wales.

I kept my gaze fixed on the summit while I climbed, trying to postpone a wider prospect until I had reached the top. Mountains do indeed exert a mystique. The remoteness of the stars may stifle their impact on the imagination; but no mountain is so remote that it cannot be reached, nor any so old that it eludes a place in Earth's pedigree. Therefore a mountain was and still is the yardstick wherewith men measure the aeons, despite the fact that the Psalmist's 'everlasting hills' are the mortal creatures of upheaval, and the mutable victims of erosion. The Greeks chose Mount Parnassus as the dwelling-place of Apollo and the Muses. On a mountain, they say, Jesus was transfigured by a mystical experience : 'And his raiment became shining, exceeding white as snow . . .' The unmystical Age of Enlightenment, by contrast, had no head for heights. When Dr Johnson climbed a modest hill in Derbyshire he was appalled 'by the horrors of the precipice . . . The ideas which it forces on the mind are, the sublime, the dreadful, the vast. Above is inaccessible altitude, below is horrible profundity.' Just so, the Sussex Downs had affrighted Cowper while he travelled to Stane Street. Wordsworth, a man of the mountains, did much to dispel the giddiness:

> ye mountains and ye lakes,
> And sounding cataracts, ye mists and winds
> Which dwell among the hills where I was born.

By this time some of the snowdrifts were a foot high, proving that I could never have walked to my original destination, along a green road over mountains higher than the Sugarloaf. But any sense of disappointment gave way to surprise and pleasure that I was able to climb this mountain, and in sunshine, too. Although I kept staring at the summit, it was impossible not to catch glimpses of the valley below and of the distant peaks beyond it. The men of those mountains had certainly been maligned, and were still misunderstood, by many of their English neighbours. Walter Savage Landor arraigned every Welshman as a robber: 'These rascals,' he growled, 'have as great a hatred of the Saxon as their runaway forefathers had. I shall never cease to wish that Julius Caesar had utterly exterminated the whole race.' Landor clearly was one of those in whom patriotism becomes an infatuated blindness to the merits of other nations. Matthew Arnold took a more civilized view: 'Wales,' he wrote, 'where the past still lives, where every place has its tradition, every name its poetry, and where the people, the genuine people, still knows this past, this tradition, this poetry, and lives with, and clings to it; while, alas, the prosperous Saxon on the other side has long forgotten his.' Welsh culture is more virile and more widespread than the Scottish. On the Abbotsford drove road I might have questioned many thousands of natives before finding one who could speak the Gaelic; but a survey in 1958 showed that Monmouthshire, an allegedly English county, still contained ten thousand people who spoke Welsh. Even more surprising, there were nearly one hundred who could not speak English. The same survey showed that in Carmarthenshire the Welsh language was spoken by 113,000 people, of whom ten thousand spoke no English at all. Such monoglots recall the old Welshwoman whom Edward Thomas met in 1910: 'She could say "Good afternoon" in English . . . Her only other English words were "beautiful" and "excursion".'

The Welsh are the most poetical of all Britons. It is possible that they are the most poetical people in the world. As the Greek populace stood spellbound before the artistry of Aeschylus, so, even today, Welsh shepherds and shopkeepers and colliers forgather at their annual festivals of Welsh art. The first recorded Eisteddfod was convened by the King of England in 1176, when the bardic crown for music went to South Wales, and that for poetry to North Wales. During the 1860s, while Parliament was trying to destroy the Welsh language, the Bardic Congress of Wales defined the purpose of an Eisteddfod as 'the eliciting of native talent, and the cherishing of love and home and honourable fame by the cultivation of poetry, music, and art'. Only a Welsh-speaker can understand the extent to which Welsh prosody imposes both a liberty and a discipline. Translation, however, does convey something of the quality of medieval Welsh lyricism:

> Maytime, fairest season,
> Loud are the birds, green the groves,
> Ploughs in furrows, ox under yoke,
> Green is the sea, sands are many-coloured . . .

But always we overhear Matthew Arnold's 'eternal note of sadness', the innate Celtic melancholy:

> At Aber Cuwag the cuckoos are calling.
> Sad it is to my mind
> That he who once heard them will hear them no more.

It is not surprising that many Scots and Welsh embraced Calvin's pessimistic parody of the teachings of Jesus. Nor is it surprising that many of them cling to their language, for when language has gone, the rest becomes an archaic national charade which the natives perform for the benefit of tourists.

Viewed from a distance, the summit of the Sugarloaf had appeared as the peak of a gradual gradient, ending at a small plateau. The gradient was certainly gradual in a Latin sense, that is, every step seemed steeper than the one before. Instead of striding to the top I walked slowly, twice pausing for breath while glancing over my shoulder. How could anyone pretend that Monmouthshire was not *de jure* Welsh? The pretence began during the reign of Henry VIII, who was descended—via a Welsh squire, Tudur ap Goronwy—from Edynfed Fychan, seneschal to Llywelyn The Great, a thirteenth-century Prince of Gwynedd. Henry, at all events, deprived the Lords Marchers of their right to try cases of robbery and murder. The Lordships were then merged into counties, to which were added the five new counties of Denbigh, Montgomery, Radnor, Brecon, and Monmouth. The English language was required of anyone aspiring to take part in public life; and Wales itself was 'incorporated, united, and annexed' as part of England. It is true that a number of Welsh gentry had asked to be annexed, but they formed only a small minority, and may have been bribed or intimidated by Thomas Cromwell, the King's chief minister. Like the Scots, therefore, the Welsh are torn between an anti-English isolationism and a measure of independence which takes an adult view of economics and defence. Also like the Scots, they have a nobility and gentry who long ago became anglicized. As John Knox boasted to Mary Queen of Scots about his English accent, so Shakespeare's Owain Glyndwr boasted to Lord Henry Percy about his English education:

> I can speak English, lord, as well as you;
> For I was trained up at the English court. . . .

Although Defoe rated Monmouthshire as English, he compared its scenery with Switzerland's: 'Here,' he wrote, 'I must mount the Alps, traverse the mountains of Wales (and indeed, they are well compar'd to the Alps in the inmost provinces). But with this exception, that in the abundance of places you have the most beautiful and pleasant valleys imaginable, and some of them, of very great extent, far exceeding the valleys so fam'd among the mountains of Savoy and Piedmont.'

The summit was now less than three hundred yards away, but some of the yards were so steep that once or twice I had to scramble up them. The wayside boulders were larger and more numerous. The grass, however, remained as richly abundant as on the lower ground. There is a difference between meadow grass and so-called turf-forming grass. The former yields hay, and is not so close-packed, because relatively few animals graze on it during the growing season. Turf-forming grass, on the other hand, produces many 'tillers' or lateral shoots, which, when grazed, send new shoots close to the surface, as well as a fibrous mass of roots several inches below the surface. Moist air, high altitude, and regular grazing ensure a rich herbage for livestock. In February, of course, most of the animals are grazing on lower and less exposed ground. The Welsh mountain sheep is a hardy and formidable-looking creature, not greatly changed since the Middle Ages, though made larger by crossing with Leicesters, Lincolns, and Downs. The rams have curled horns, and yellowish legs and faces. The wool is white and short; the mutton, lean and of prime quality.

About twenty yards short of the summit I looked back on the way I had come. As along the Scottish drove road, the impression was of a huge golf course and on it the darker green of the road. But neither in Scotland nor on Dartmoor had I been so conscious of the height, the spaciousness. In Scotland the switchback tended to hide the hinterland; on Dartmoor the Way entered several ravines. Here, on the Sugarloaf Mountain, I felt as though I were within twenty yards of the roof of the world. But those twenty yards really were heavy going. My venerable dog looked up now and again, as if to remind me that we were not so young as we used to be. Then with a final spurt we reached the top, the plateau; and there at last we received our reward, pressed down and overflowing. The Brecon Beacons shone, and the Black Mountains likewise, those sterile sandstone shapes; all snow-tipped against a sky whose brilliance was heightened by three white clouds hovering above the peaks, like extensions of the snow. Fortunately, the high peaks hid Ebbw Vale, a region long ago ravaged by industry. In 1854 George Borrow described the Vale as 'a singular mixture of nature and art, of the voices of birds and clanking of chains, of the mists of heaven and the smoke of furnaces'. At about that same time a Government Commission revealed some home truths concerning the blessings of the new machine age: 'The employment of children of seven was common,' it stated, 'and in many pits children were employed at six, in some at five, and in one case a child of three was found to be employed.' And what was their employment? They crouched at the bottom of a coal mine, opening and shutting doors by pulling a string: 'These doors,' the Commission explained, 'were in the charge of a little boy or girl, who sat in a small hole, with a string in his or her hand, in darkness and solitude for twelve hours or longer at a time.'

The appalling conditions in Ebbw Vale and elsewhere bred a herd of dangerous livestock, the so-called 'Scotch Cattle', a gang of Monmouthshire workmen who blacked their faces, and were led by a 'bull' wearing the skins of a wild beast. Operating chiefly at night, the gang robbed, injured, and sometimes murdered anyone who opposed their violent attack on the employers. It is significant that very few of the gang were native Welshmen. One of their leaders came from Staffordshire, and conveniently disappeared when a constable had been murdered. Another leader was a Frenchman from the Paris mob. The 'Scotch Cattle' were followed by the Monmouthshire Physical Force Chartists, with headquarters at the Coach and Horses Inn at Blackwood. In 1839 three armed mobs converged on Pontypool, but were dispersed by troops.

Poverty, however, no longer pursues the colliers and steel workers of Ebbw Vale, most of whom earn at least twice as much as a farmhand, while some earn three times as much. Nevertheless, the shame and horror of those distant days still linger in the memory, and the men who witnessed them still speak from the past. Thomas Carlyle, for instance, was dismissed as a sentimentalist because he did not unreservedly support Britain's export drive: 'British industrial existence,' he protested, 'seems fast becoming one huge poison swamp of reeking pestilence physical and moral ... a hideous *living* Golgotha of souls and bodies buried alive ...' One day, perhaps, a man will no longer be dismissed as a sentimentalist when he questions the benefits of a revolution whereby England turned herself into a factory, and the factory hands into bored and potentially dangerous robots .

Then the invisible apparition vanished, and I found myself gazing down at the middle distance, where the white farms and cottages might have been snowdrifts, so spaced as to fulfil St Patrick's condition for good neighbourliness: 'Not near enough to create familiarity, nor far enough to prevent company.' Never before had I seen Wales in such radiant width and depth and height. The peaks rose up unwearied, and were white. The valleys lay at peace, and were green. So, in the end, February had granted me a sunlit winterscape, framed in snow. It was the *summum bonum* of all my journeys along the green roads of Britain.

The descent from the summit offered a new prospect and a different perspective, which I was at leisure to admire while loping where I so lately had scrambled. And still the sky was slashed with white peaks to the north and with white hills to the south, shining all the way to Monmouth and the high ground at Trelleck. Were those hills snow-covered when Defoe compared them with the Swiss Alps? Before leaving the stillness, I looked back at the domed mountain, and then further, to its distant peers, with the mind's eye remembering former journeys across the Black Mountains and along the old drove road from Tregaron into the heart of solitude; and to every peak and every valley I extended Sir William Watson's greeting:

> Wild Wales, whose kindred swayed
> This island, ages ere an English word
> Was breathed in Britain, let an Englishman
> Hail and salute you . . .

The Inkpen Ridgeway

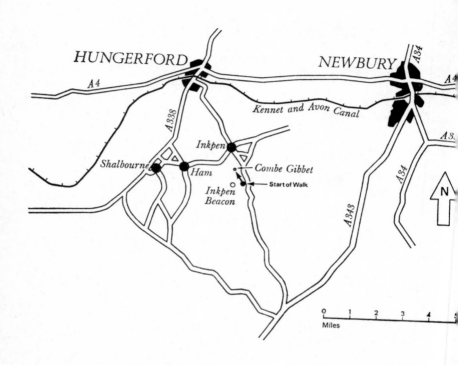

9 The Inkpen Ridgeway

CLIMBING head-bent against wind and mist, I did not see The Thing until I was within a few yards of it. Then I halted, as though a wire had been stretched across the path. Alone on a green mound stood a gallows, etched against a wild sky. Suddenly the wind seemed to echo the grim chords with which Berlioz opened his *March to the Scaffold*. 'That,' I muttered, 'settles it.' And back I went, down the sodden track, into the world of the living.

This time the weather really had failed me, or perhaps it would be fairer to say that it had fooled the forecasters. The previous day's prediction was for 'occasional showers in the afternoon'. Showers, however, are among winter's less daunting features, unlikely to deter a countryman from walking. I therefore decided to take them in my stride. The first of the 'occasional showers in the afternoon' began while I was breakfasting at a hotel. The second began while I was driving to the green road. The third did not begin at all, because the second continued until I had reached my destination, where it became a deluge. I heartily agreed with a report to the Board of Agriculture in 1794, which stated that on these Downs 'the climate ... is so well known for its coldness and keenness, as to be almost proverbial'. Meanwhile, hoping that the sky would soon clear, I took the first step on a Wessex ridgeway, straight into a foot of water, the road at that point being rutted as well as steep. After about four hundred yards the steepness slackened a little, and I felt sufficiently interested to look up from my circumnavigation of the potholes. It was then that I saw The Thing. In fairness, however, I must confess that the weather itself had already tempted me to retreat, for instead of looking down on Berkshire and Wiltshire, I was peering into a mist.

Six months later I tried again, choosing a spell of fine weather in June. My approach to the Ridgeway led through Inkpen, whose name has nothing whatever to do with authorship, but is a tautological version of the Saxon *ing* and the Celtic *pen*, each meaning 'hill'. When I first knew it, Inkpen was a remote village at the foot of the Berkshire Downs, only a mile or two from Wiltshire, and less than five from Hampshire. Today the place has acquired a rash of modern houses, some of which are occupied only at weekends. Astride a knoll beyond the village, the church has a lych-gate, a tiled bell tower, and some thirteenth-century windows. A few yards away, on higher ground, stands an eighteenth-century rectory. On lower ground stands a venerable farmhouse. This is the best of Inkpen, a steep and sylvan scene, graced by close-cropped grass above a narrow lane which soon joins a wider one to Inkpen Beacon alias Combe Gibbet.

In brilliant sunshine I drove along the wider lane, up hills that were bare of everything except grass and a few chalk tracks. After a mile or so I sighted the Inkpen Ridgeway descending from the left, then crossing the lane, and then climbing to the Beacon. Once more I parked the car near the crossing, and once more stepped into a rut, though this one was so sunbaked that it felt more like granite than chalk. For all I knew, it was the same rut that had baptized me ankle-deep during my previous visit. But what a transformation! Instead of a shrill wind galloping from the north, a quiet breeze sauntered from the south. Instead of rain drenching the mist, sunlight polished the grass. Larks sang their sky-high Matins, and the green road grew wider than the metalled lane. In autumn and winter the Ridgeway is used only by farmhands and a few intrepid walkers; but in summertime it attracts motorists, of whom the sillier sort drive through pot-holes to the summit. Fortunately, however, the average motorist is neither an early riser nor a weekday walker. This being a Wednesday, and the hour 9 a.m., the Beacon in June was as peaceful as the Sugarloaf in February. One need not be a civil engineer in order to understand why the chalk-based Ridgeway was now in prime condition, grassy and springy and dry. If metalled surfaces are neglected, their paving is soon cracked by frost, whereas green roads thrive on frost because it crumbles the soil and thereby encourages the herbage. Moreover, chalk and limestone drain themselves easily, whereas a modern road will quickly disintegrate if its culverts are not cleared. The Romans did clear their culverts, and when the Saxons failed to do likewise, the surfaces were eroded.

The word 'ridgeway' comes from the Old English *hrycweg*, meaning 'a road that follows a ridge or hilltop'. Such roads are plentiful in Berkshire, Hampshire, Dorset, and Wiltshire. Thus, the Great Ridgeway began near Streatly, only a few miles south of the Icknield Way, and proceeded via Marlborough and Shaftesbury to Uplyme in Devon. The Dorset Coastal Ridgeway can be traced from Swanage to Abbotsbury; the Harrow Ridgeway, from Hampshire to Somerset. All these ridgeways were used by pedlars, and some by pilgrims to the shrines at Avebury and Stonehenge. The pedlars carried wares from distant parts. The Great Ridgeway, for instance, has yielded flint from Norfolk, beads from Egypt, copper from Ireland, tin from Cornwall, jet from Yorkshire, amber from the Baltic, and gold from Wales.

This time The Thing did *not* take me by surprise. But it still looked out of place, all the more so because it stood in such lonely surroundings. I went up to it, and touched the timber. Put not your trust in guidebooks that are based on other guidebooks. For example, my winter visit was darkened by thoughts of the criminals who (said the guidebook) had been hanged there. On reflection, however, I began to doubt the guide. Men were indeed hanged publicly, but at a place where many passers-by would see and take heed. Why, then, was a gibbet erected on a track which only a few farmfolk followed? Consulting a second guidebook, I learned again that highwaymen and other criminals had perished on Combe Gibbet; that the gibbet itself was three centuries old; and that the owners or holders of the site were required to maintain The Thing in good condition. Since the timber was relatively modern, I took some trouble to discover the truth, as follows: the present gibbet *is* relatively modern; the original was erected in 1676; and the only execution on it occurred during the same year, when a couple were hanged for adultery and murder. Combe Gibbet is both grisly and bogus, neither meriting preservation nor enhancing beauty. I wished heartily that it had shared the fate of the gibbet which Thomas Hardy mentioned in his diary: 'Jack White's gibbet [near Wincanton] was standing as late as 1835—i.e. the oak-post with the iron arm sticking out, and a portion of the cage in which the body had formerly hung. It could have been standing now if some young men had not burnt it down by piling faggots round it one fifth of November.'

Turning away from the misplaced monument, I looked northward over a vast plain rippled with small hills, and backed by a blue smudge on the horizon. In the middle distance were farms, houses, rivers, roads, churches, woods, barns. With map and glasses I was able to identify some of the place-names, each one the work of practical poets, the kind of men who had baptized Sliding Hill near the Icknield Way: Hell Corner, Cold Harbour, Oaken Copse, Crooked Soley, Mount Prosperous, Marriage Hill, Great Hidden Farm, and South Hidden Farm (which stood five miles north of its Great namesake). Beyond those places I saw the Kennet and Avon Canal; further yet, the Marlborough Downs and the Lambourn Downs; and finally that blue smudge, the Cotswolds. Everything glistened in sunlight, and some things winked, notably a distant window and the metal of moving cars. Turning south, I found the vista less expansive though not less pleasing. The hills and wooded combes were full of surprises. No house appeared there. So far as I recall, no building of any sort appeared. It was all grassland and cornfields, birdsong and woods, peace and prosperity (unless you happened to be a farmer struggling for existence on a couple of hundred acres). As recently as 1950 the population of Wiltshire was little more than 800,000 or one person to approximately three acres; and only three of its towns contained more than 10,000 people.

Just beyond the gibbet the Ridgeway threatened to lose itself in a maze of rubbish and stagnant pools. By skirting the impasse I regained the road, which soon became wide and clearly defined, with trees on the left and the plain on the right. After several switchbacks the road levelled, this time passing two small woods on the right, in the second of which stood a prehistoric burial site, marking the boundary with Wiltshire. During King Offa's reign the Ridgeway lay in Wessex, the kingdom of the West Saxons. Both the kingdom and the name became obsolete, like those of Mercia and Northumbria, and they remained obsolete for a thousand years, when Thomas Hardy revived the name by co-opting the kingdom as the background of his novels. Although he was a Dorset man, Hardy never used the word 'Dorset' in his books (except, if I remember, as a footnote). Nor did he name any of the six counties in his fictitious topography. All became parts of Wessex, a name which he first used in *Far From the Madding Crowd*: 'I am reminded,' he wrote, 'that it was in the chapters of "Far From the Madding Crowd" as they appeared month by month in a popular magazine, that I first ventured to adopt the word "Wessex" from the pages of early English history, and give it a fictitious significance as the existing name of the district once included in the extinct kingdom.' He then added: 'The region designated was known but vaguely, and I was often asked even by educated people where it lay.' In 1878, when Smith and Elder were about to publish *The Return of the Native*, Hardy wrote to them as follows: 'I enclose a sketch-map of the supposed scene in which *The Return of the Native* is laid, copied from the one I used in writing the story; and my suggestion is that we place the engraving of it as a frontispiece to the first

volume.' Nearly a century later the map was still included in
the novels; not, however, as Hardy had suggested, on a
frontispiece, but at the back of the book, where some readers
found it too late. Hardy's map, at all events, divided Wessex
into seven parts, stretching eastward from Lower Wessex
(Cornwall) to North Wessex (Berkshire). Some of the map's
place-names are real—Plymouth, for instance, and Bath—
but the places that appear in the novels are given pen-names
(Exmoor becomes Exon Moor, and Oxford becomes Christ-
minster). In a more personal vein, Hardy named one of his
dogs Wessex, and wrote an elegiac poem about him.

At the western edge of the second wood I entered Wiltshire, a county which is remembered thrice each year when,
at the end of term, the boys of Marlborough School sing a
song to remind themselves that even they will grow old, but
that the pains of age will be eased whenever they return to
Wiltshire:

> Ah, then we'll cry, Thank God! my lads,
> The Kennet's running still;
> And see! the old White Horse still pads
> Up there on Granham Hill.

On the hill above Abbotsford, you remember, I walked
shirtless and barefoot, thinking it unlikely that anyone would
be there to notice such eccentricity. I was mistaken. On
Combe Hill I walked shirted and shod, thinking it very
likely indeed that several people *would* be there to approve
my correctness. And again I was mistaken. Not since leaving
Inkpen had I seen a soul; and even there the soul was indoors, sustaining its substantiality with bacon and eggs. Yet
this was June, a month when many Britons took their annual holiday. So, I proceeded in sartorial solitude, along a
wide and grassy road, with larks overhead, blackbirds all
around, and on my right a vision of southern England, briefly
hidden by two woods and rising ground. I was well into my
stride when the rising ground gave way, just enough to reveal the roofs of Ham, about a couple of miles to the north-

west, and several hundred feet below the Ridgeway, which
showed no desire at all to enter Ham, but turned south-west,
zig-zagging over Ham Hill. Then came a bald sector, where
tractors and climate had eroded the turf. After that, the road
passed a may tree, reminding me of Offa's Dyke. On the
right, a herd of Guernseys peered over the barbed wire.
Guernseys may properly be called romantic creatures because the breed was born several centuries ago, when a
Guernsey girl married a Jersey man, each bringing one of
their native calves as part of the dowry. Channel Islanders
believe that one of the calves was an Isigny from Normandy,
and that the other was a Froment de Leon from Guernsey.
Like their owners, the calves mated, which explains why
Jerseys and Guernseys share certain characteristics. Since
1789 the Island of Jersey has banned all live cattle except its
own, and a later law has banned all except Guernseys from
Guernsey. Moreover, once an animal has been exported, it
is never allowed to return home. The so-called Alderney
breed is a misnomer because Guernseys are the only cattle on
Alderney. As the milk of both breeds contains a high fat-
content, you will often see one or two of them in a herd of
Friesians, whose milk, although abundant, is deficient in fat.
Guernseys are larger and less elegant than Jerseys, but still
exceedingly handsome, with creamy nose, amber-coloured
hooves, and a fawn coat that is sometimes dappled with what
the breeders call 'orange and lemon'.

At the next field the land on the right fell away abruptly,
showing Savernake Forest and the small woods that once
formed part of it: Foxbury Wood, Chisbury Wood, How
Wood, Noke Wood, Bloxham Copse, Lingfield Copse, Lawn
Coppice, Park Coppice. The road was running level now,
wider than ever, flanked by a tall hedgerow on the left. There
I rested, pillowed not by primroses, as along the Icknield
Way, but by one of the innumerable mole-hills that abound
on chalk downs. Despite the absence of human beings, I still
found myself the centre of attraction because the Guernseys
had wandered down from the other field, and were now star-

ing at me with that stolidity which tempts one to wonder what the animals are thinking, for something recognizable as thought must surely afflict the higher forms of life. Beyond those Guernseys the view was easy to describe, yet difficult to place. None of the fields was especially large nor noticeably small. Most of them were neatly hedged. The husbandry was part arable and part livestock. 'Wiltshire,' said William Camden, 'is altogether a mediterranean or mid land county ...' He did not mean, of course, that Wiltshire is a Midland county, but rather that—unlike Devon and Lincolnshire—it is entirely surrounded by land. Now there are certain regions which a travelled Englishman can place easily and accurately. Dartmoor is one; Fenland, another; Breckland, a third. All such regions may be identified positively via their crops, contours, climate, architecture. The landscape of the Inkpen Ridgeway, however, required a negative definition. The abundance of trees, for instance, suggested that I was not in north Cornwall; the thatched roofs suggested that I was not in north Derbyshire; the spaciousness suggested that I was not in north Surrey. Yet no single feature supplied a positive clue; no gritstone mill, as in Lancashire; no smoke-smeared skyline, as in Staffordshire; no towering summit, as in Westmorland. However, the advanced state of the flora and the domesticated appearance of the fields did suggest that this was southern England, though not the level Shires, nor the tawny Cotswolds, nor the beechen Chilterns. By piecing together the thatched roofs, the stone and brick houses, the shapes of the hills, and the tones of the talk ... by such means a traveller would probably set the scene as the south-eastern edge of the west country. If he were uncommonly knowledgeable he would be uncannily accurate: 'This,' he would say, 'is Wiltshire. Length fifty-four miles. Breadth thirty-seven. Shape roughly oblong. Position on the map, approximately vertical.'

From the hospitable mole-hill, I followed the Ridgeway's gradual descent, passing on the left a track to Town Farm, a handsome homestead, perched on a plateau above the green road. I ventured along that track in order to recollect an invisible hamlet and a happy memory which began thus: once upon a time, during my very first visit to Inkpen, long before I knew that I would ever write about the place, I said to an Inkpenner: 'How far away is Hampshire?' He replied: 'Three miles.' He was nearly right. The lane, I remember, went uphill and down, into woods and then out of them, around bends and then more bends; in parts an unfenced and hedgeless lane, where corn grew within a yard of any vehicle that passed, if any ever did. It was, you understand, a magical lane, seen on one of those magical mornings when May tempts you to suppose that you have taken leave of your senses, and are in Arcady, or Paradise, or some other Region of the Blest. So strong was the illusion that I took a photograph of the lane, as proof of a journey through fairyland. If at this point you do not understand what I am talking about, you have my sympathy; but I shall proceed nevertheless, into Hampshire and Linkenholt, a hamlet so secluded that I wondered whether anyone else had come to it, except the present heirs and successors of the first-founders. I counted six cottages at Linkenholt, and then gave up because there were no more to be counted, or none that I could see to count. The small church resembled an islet in a graveyard whose vastness seemed to account for the silence, all the inhabitants being dead and buried. Yet one at least of the cottages seemed to be in good condition. It was a miniature cottage, beautifully proportioned to fit a race of Little People. Just then my dog barked at a cat, and the sound ran throughout the universe. When the echo had faded, a tottery old man emerged and stood stooping in the low doorway. He must at some period have seen another human being, because he said to me: 'What is the time?' I felt tempted to answer: 'They have just sighted the Armada.' Instead, I was honest. 'I do not know the time,' I replied, 'because I carry no watch, because I feel no haste. Such has long been my custom when engaged on an important task. At present,' I explained, 'I am busy doing nothing in particular.'

'My father,' said the cottager, 'was fond of fishing. Have you come here?' And then he went indoors, like the man on a Darby and Joan clock, and in some ways like the man on a bicycle beside the Kennet and Avon Canal. This grieved me because I wished to ask many questions about Linkenholt. When I got home I looked it up in a book, which is not at all the same as writing it down on the spot. The first book told me what I already knew: 'Linkenholt is chiefly a collection of farm buildings.' The second book told me something else I knew: 'OE *hlinca-holt* "wood on the hills".' Perhaps it was as well. I saw Linkenholt as I shall never see it again, when the year and I were young; and that must suffice.

Emerging from those memories, I continued along the Ridgeway, which was now wider than ever. It passed some fir trees on the left and then it dipped a few hundred yards before levelling out and crossing a lane that led down-hill to Ham, a couple of miles away. Ham being the village nearest to the Ridgeway, I went there, and found it alto-gether delightful, except for one thing. The handful of houses stood among trees and roadside grass. Every one of them was either old or in some other way suitable. Ham, in short, justified its Old English name, which means 'home-stead', or 'manor', or 'village'. At the end of a drive I found the medieval church with an embattled tower, some panelled box-pews, and a pulpit that looked as though it had been part of a three-decker. A yew tree in the churchyard was so plump that I used my belt as a tape measure with which to span the girth; nearly nineteen feet. Behind the church I found an eighteenth-century manor house with a bell gable, all gleaming white in the sun. Noticing that my dog was try-ing to lap a parched puddle, I went up to one of the cottages, where a woman was trimming the wayside grass. In no time at all she produced a bowl of water. When I felicitated her on living in such a peaceful place, she replied that the place was not at all peaceful. This puzzled me until five fast cars flashed by, pursued by a black-jerkined motor-cyclist. 'They're going to the gliding club,' the woman explained, pointing up at the hills. That was the one reason why Ham is not altogether delightful.

Back on the Ridgeway again, I observed the effects of constant use and relative neglect, for whereas the previous sector was wide and in places worn, the next sector was narrow and comparatively smooth. Sheltered by a hedge on the left, the road resembled the narrowest segments of Stane Street, as level and straight as Bunyan's: 'Look before thee, dost thou see this narrow way ... it is as straight as a rule can make it. This is the way thou must go.' Here, I felt, the pedlars and the drovers had made up for time lost while climbing Inkpen Beacon and the hills en route to Town Farm. Happening to look back at the farm, I noticed some sarsen stones glinting in the sun. Sarsens are the hardest relics of a layer that once covered the chalk hills, but had long since been eroded. The medieval Wessex folk called them Saracens because they looked grim and alien among chalk and grass. Later generations called them Grey Wethers. Exposed by the climate, the stones were used by the Celts who built Avebury and Stonehenge, and by the later generations who built churches and houses on the downs. 'Down', by the way, seems a strange name for land that conspicuously goes up. In fact, the word comes from the Celtic *dun* or *din*, meaning 'hill'. In Domesday Book the name of Inkpen appeared as *Ingepene*, though its application to this Ridgeway is a relatively modern device of topographers. Some of the green roads, however, acquired their name during the Middle Ages and perhaps during the Dark Ages; names such as Ox Way, White Way, Salt Way, Sugar Way. The Salt and White Ways were used by traders in salt. Sugar was unknown to primitive mankind, but salt was a common medicine and preservative. During the Middle Ages it achieved symbolic importance as a social barrier at table; gentlefolk sat above the salt; groundlings, below it. The word 'salary' comes from *salarium*, an allowance granted to Roman soldiers for buying their salt ration. The word ultimately became a synonym for soldiers' pay. We still speak of a shiftless fellow as 'not worth his salt'.

Midway along the straight and narrow sector, I passed a wood on the left, not a great distance from New Buildings, which were not new at all. It is remarkable, the number of houses that still bear a name they received centuries ago. At Stratford-upon-Avon the world flocks to see New Place, which was already decaying when Shakespeare bought it for £60. Newbuildings Place, near Shipley in Sussex, was the home of Wilfred Scawen Blunt, who wrote an account of its long history. Oxford's New College was founded six centuries ago; and near Edward Gibbon's ancestral seat at Gawcot in Buckinghamshire stands the New Inn, likewise several centuries old.

After about nine furlongs of arrow-like straightness, the Ridgeway reached the end of Rivar Hill, but then dropped south-west to avoid climbing it. Ever since Inkpen Beacon the road had tried to avoid both the highest and the lowest ground. There were times when it appeared to align itself on various prehistoric sites, including a long barrow on the Beacon; several tumuli in the wood that marked the Wiltshire boundary; an earthwork just south of this narrow sector; and, further on, another barrow and two more tumuli. Which, I wondered, came first, the road, or the sites? If the sites came first, there may be some validity in a book by Alfred Watkins, called *The Old Straight Track*, which was published in 1927, as an attempt to prove that many green roads really are aligned on conspicuous landmarks. The question, wrote the author, 'is whether it is a humanly designed fact ... that mounds, moats, beacons, and mark stones fall into straight lines throughout Britain, with fragmentary evidence of trackways on the alignments'. Looking first at the Ridgeway and then at the map, I allowed that this road did seem to be aligned on beacons and burial sites. George Borrow certainly believed that Celtic burial sites 'were afterwards used as strongholds, bonhills, or beaconheights'. In a note about the topography of *Treasure Island*, Stevenson cited the relation between tracks and landmarks: 'The names, the shapes of woodlands, the curves of the rivers, the prehistoric footsteps of men still distinctly traceable up hill and down dale, the mills, the ruins, the ponds, and the ferries, perhaps the *Standing Stones* and/or the *Druidic Circle* . . . here is an inexhaustible fund of interest.'

By this time the sun was warming my left cheek, and I decided that it was time for coffee and sandwiches. So, I sat down, and served them. Half-way through the second cup I heard a car screeching up a lane, less than half a mile westwards. A glance at the map confirmed the truth of the Ham complaint. Somewhere nearby was a gliding club. But the worst was yet to come, not from the lane but from the sky, where an aircraft began to tow a glider, droning like a wasp on a window. Then the nuisance returned. Then it reappeared, towing another glider. And so the noise continued, disturbing many people for many miles around. Is there, I wondered, any place in Britain, at which a man can nowadays feel safe from builders and motors and aircraft? The voice of John Ruskin answered *ex tenebris* : 'Wherever I travel in England, I find that men have no other desire or hope, but to have large houses and to move fast. Every perfect and lovely spot which they can touch they defile.'

After what seemed a very long time the aircraft ran out of cargoes. Peace returned while the gliders played like Icarus, though without venturing so close to the sun. Prompted by the stillness, I asked another question: is May more delightful than June? Along Offa's Dyke I would have answered: 'Yes.' If pressed to justify the answer, I would have said: 'In May the young leaves are at their freshest. Bluebells surge like inland seas. The birds are as blithe as in April, and more numerous. Summer waits ahead.' But now, along the Inkpen Ridgeway, I revised my answer, saying: 'In June the sun is stronger, the days are longer, the nights are warmer, the flowers are gayer. One can swim in the sea without shivering; and the mowers are at work, reaping the year's first harvest.'

Beyond Rivar Hill the road followed the line of Rivar Down, a spur of high ground, sweeping south-west for nearly two miles. At the sharpest point of the arc the road crossed a lane coming up from Shalbourne, two miles away; and thither I went. Shalbourne is larger and less compact than Ham. The Saxons named it after the *scealda burn* or 'shallow stream' that flows nearby. Most of the houses are either red-bricked or half-timbered, and several are thatched. The re-built church contains some features from the original Norman building, as well as a memorial to Sir Francis Choke: 'Praye Ye Al for the Sole of Francis Choke—Descessed in the Yere of Oure Lord A 1562.' The date is interesting because it shows the extent to which the Reformation was both a political and a theological revolt. Thirty years earlier, in 1533, Convocation had joined with the Universities of Oxford and Cambridge in asserting that 'the bishop of Rome has no more authority in England than any other foreign Bishop'. Only three years before that declaration, an Act of Supremacy had asserted that the Crown was 'Supreme in all causes as well ecclesiastical as civil.' The King himself, Henry VIII, had in his younger days written a tract, *Assertio septem Sacramentorum*, upholding the Church against its Lutheran opponents, for which the Pope bestowed on him a title that his heirs and successors still bear, *Fidei Defensor* (Defender of the Faith). Yet in 1562 the villagers at Shalbourne were still observing the medieval custom of praying for the souls of the departed. Moreover, the departed himself had been given a medieval tomb with pillared canopy and an effigy showing him pillowed on his helmet, while his feet rested on a lion. Robert Bridges saw a similar effigy in just such a church:

> So fair the characters
> With which the dusty scroll
> That tells his title, stirs
> A requiem for his soul.

The return from Shalbourne to the Ridgeway was steep, and at the end of it I looked for a cool place where I might sip the last half-cup of coffee while the dog drank from his saucer. I found the cool place in a copse on the far side of the

Scottish drove road, Selkirkshire

Abbotsford, Sir Walter Scott's house near Melrose

Savernake Forest

Conservation work on the Kennet and Avon canal, Hungerford

Kennet and Avon canal, Pewsey

Sugarloaf Mountain, Abergavenny

Ham Common on the Inkpen Ridgeway

Inkpen Church

St Gennys Church, Cornwall

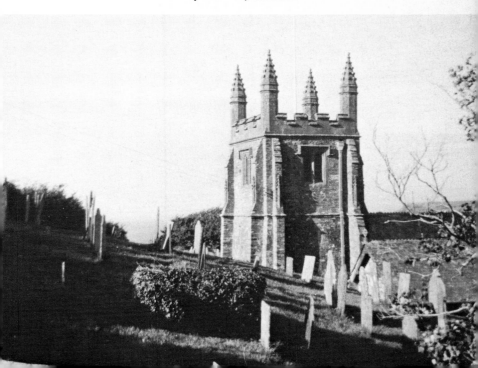

The Inkpen Ridgeway, approaching River Hill

Farmhouse at St Gennys

Coombe Valley, Morwenstow

Cliff Path, near Bude

Cornish Coast Path near St Gennys

Shalbourne lane, and there we rested, watching the sunlight as it filtered through the leaves overhead. The hour was four o'clock or thereabouts, the zenith of the heat of the day. Along the Scottish drove road I had not needed to people the grass with imaginary travellers. They came of their own accord. But on this tract the Ridgeway showed neither footprint nor hoofmark. Therefore I could only imagine a fur-clad figure striding barefoot between the trees; on his back a load of merchandise, and in his hand a spear or bow, ready for use against wolves, bison, boars. Matthew Arnold described as 'dark Iberians' the men with whom that fur-clad figure had done business on the shore, perhaps on the Norfolk shore, whence he was travelling via the Icknield Way to Wiltshire and the far west. Like many another Briton, the trader may have been too timid to confront the visiting merchants. Instead, he set his goods on the beach and then hid nearby, watching to see what kind of goods the strangers would set there in return:

> through sheets of foam
> Shy traffickers, the dark Iberians, come;
> And on the beach undid his corded bales.

The descendants of those 'shy traffickers' were among Maurice Hewlett's neighbours when he lived in Wiltshire during the early years of the twentieth century: 'We are all Iberians here,' he wrote, 'a swarthy people, dark-haired, grey-eyed, rather under than over the mean height. The aboriginal strain has proved itself strong, and we are neolithic chiefly on the distaff side.'

As relics of the Iberians, a long barrow and several tumuli stood close to where I was sitting. Their nature and purpose varied with their age, as did the method of burial. During the Neolithic Age, from 3400 to 1600 BC, many of the long barrows were rectangular mounds, about ten feet high and three hundred feet long. Some contained only two corpses; others, more than twenty. During the Early Bronze Age, from 1600 to 1400 BC, inhumanition gave way to cremation.

The bodies of important Wessex people were as a rule placed in round barrows; the men under a large mound, the women under a small, known respectively as bell-barrows and disc-barrows. The people of the Neolithic Age were more advanced than those of the Palaeolithic or Old Stone Age. They could, for instance, perform trepanation or brain surgery by means of a sharpened flint. During the Bronze Age a highly individual craftsmanship arose in Wessex, producing weapons and ornaments for a rich élite.

Since leaving Inkpen Beacon the Ridgeway had passed within a mile or so of six prehistoric sites, yet the map showed large areas, far to the north, without any such sites. This lent weight to the theory that many green roads really were aligned on ancient monuments. Meanwhile, continuing its south-westerly curve, the road came within easy walking distance of a later legacy, the Roman. Away to the north, in the depths of Castle Copse, stood the site of a Roman villa; and since every Roman villa stood within reasonable distance from a Roman road, I was not surprised that the map marked just such a road, running from the outskirts of Marlborough, through Savernake Forest, and then, near Tidcombe, indulging a series of curves, first to the south-east, then to the east, in order to avoid a deep valley at Hippenscombe. From Tottenham House the road crossed the line of the canal that Rennie was to build, whereafter it survived as a metalled lane until it disappeared near Wilton. This road may date from AD 43, when Vespian led the Second Augustan Legion across southern England. The road itself was no great distance from Cirencester or *Corinium*, once the second largest city in Britain, only a few miles from the Thames and its barges downstream to London and the Channel and Gaul. So, not for the first time on my journeys, I felt the presence of a civilization which Hilaire Belloc acknowledged as the basis of Englishry. Yet the ultimate aura was prehistoric, for if Stane Street crossed the nursery of Saxon England, then the Inkpen Ridgeway crossed the seed-bed of Celtic Britain. Defoe underestimated the truth when he declared that Wiltshire contained 'three hundred and fifty ancient encampments and fortifications'. Recent archaeology has added greatly to the discoveries of eighteenth-century antiquaries.

If you include certain unrecorded strolls before breakfast, then at Inkpen, and then again at Ham and Shalbourne, I had already walked the better part of twenty miles, up steep hills and under a hot sun. Nevertheless, the weather was so inviting that I strode in rhythm with Handel's advice to the daughter of Zion, that she should 'rejoice greatly'. And while I strode, I rediscovered a profound commonplace, namely, that there is a limit to the number of facts which can be acquired; a limit to the number which can be recalled from memory, and a limit to the number which can be simultaneously assembled and assessed; but there seems no limit at all to the wisdom which sometimes prompts a fact-finder to bask in the sun, assimilating impressions rather than details, and sensations rather than thoughts. Once again, therefore, I rested by the way. In fact, I fell asleep, and the dog likewise.

When I awoke, the sun stood at seven of the clock. The air felt as warm as ever. Cuckoos and blackbirds were loud calendars. The last half-mile of the journey was passed in what I can only describe as a vigorous daze. To start with, I reminded myself of the gradual evolution of the land around me, its reclamation from forest and scrub and swamp; its Celtic mounds, Roman roads, Saxon cots, Norman castles, Tudor churches, Stuart manors, Georgian rectories, Atomic pylons. But the centuries soon faded. It was enough to hear the birds, to smell the grass, to feel the sun.

Emerging from some trees, the Ridgeway reached a lane and then vanished. On the far side of the lane, in a wood, I could find only a recent cart-rut. Why the road disappeared there, whether and in what direction it proceeded further, was a mystery and likely to remain so, unless a second Edward Thomas discovered a route to Llanymawddwy. But I did not complain. Throughout most of a June day I had walked and talked and wandered and slept, with never a cloud to be seen, and only a few noisome toys to be heard in passing. So, I went slowly downhill, with the sun stroking the nape of my neck; back to the world of transport and accommodation and dog-grooming.

The North Cornish Coast

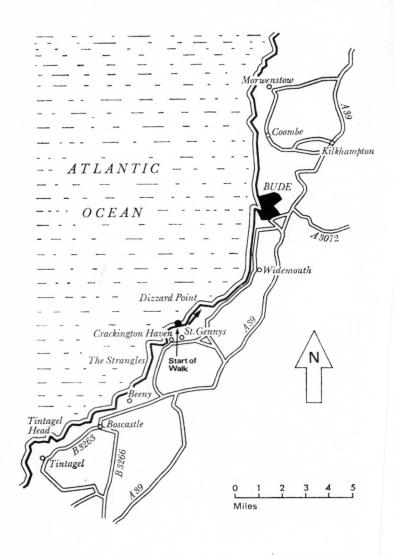

ATLANTIC

OCEAN

Morwenstow

Coombe

Kilkhampton

A 39

BUDE

A 3072

Widemouth

Dizzard Point

A 39

Crackington Haven St. Gennys

Start of Walk

The Strangles

Beeny

Tintagel Head

Boscastle

B 3263

B 3266

Tintagel

A 39

N

| 0 | 1 | 2 | 3 | 4 | 5 |

Miles

S T Gennys is a hamlet within sight of the Atlantic. In order to get there I drove along the main road south from Bude, hemmed in by mobile caravans that crawled up the hills and then careered down the dales, swaying as they sped. Time, in short, had fulfilled a prophecy which was made by *The Cornish Magazine* nearly a century ago: 'Unless Cornishmen look to it, their country will be spoiled before they know it.' After a few dangerous miles I forsook the car queue, following a narrow lane to St Gennys, whose name recalls the heavenly and multitudinous host who are said to have converted Cornwall *ex partibus infidelium*. Not all of those conversions are accepted as valid. When, for example, Cardinal Newman was a Fellow of Oriel, he invited J. A. Froude, another Oriel don, to write a life of St Neot. Froude accepted, but issued a *caveat emptor*: 'In the lives of the Christian saints,' he warned, 'the order of nature seems only to have existed to give holy men an opportunity of showing their superiority to material conditions.' How right he was. St Gennys or Genesius was a French martyr who, having been beheaded, picked up the missing part, tucked it under one arm, and kept it there for the rest of his life. But Gennys was no match for the miraculous St Patrick, who is said to have kindled a fire with an icicle, changed a brigand into a wolf, and sailed the seas on an altar stone.

The lane to St Gennys crossed a land of drystone walls and windswept loneliness. In 1870, when Thomas Hardy came this way by night, the scene was even lonelier: 'Scarcely a solitary house or man,' he wrote, 'had been visible along the whole dreary distance of open country. The only lights apparent on earth were some spots of dull red, glowing here and there upon the distant hills, smouldering fires for the consumption of peat and gorse-roots.' Had he travelled by day, I felt, Hardy would not have dismissed the scene as 'dreary'. It was rugged and bleak indeed, but far too bracing to seem dreary.

After much meandering, the lane descended into St Gennys, and there it ended. The only buildings were a disused school, a small farmhouse, and a Norman church. Beyond them the Atlantic reflected a cloudless September sky. Once again the British climate had smiled on my pilgrimage, for this was *dies mirabilis*; September, in fact, sunny and serene. St Gennys church was a typically Cornish amalgam of Norman gauntness, Perpendicular plainness, and skilful siting in a hollow below the lane, sheltered from Atlantic gales. The churchyard was so steep that one of its paths rose almost to the level of the church roof. The dumpy Norman tower just peered above the further slope, offering views of the sea. Five centuries ago the upper parts of the tower were blown away and then restored, this time with buttresses. The Norman chancel was built of Tintagel greenstone.

My first task was to find the green road itself, part of a Cornwall Coast Path from Marsland Mouth near Bude to Cremyll near Torpoint, which was formally opened in 1973, as part of the Peninsula Coast Path from Minehead in Somerset to Poole in Dorset, a distance of 515 miles. In the words of the Countryside Commission, this green track consists of 'continuous rights of way offering opportunities for ... extensive journeys' untroubled by traffic. While I was consulting the map a man appeared, driving five cows. 'The parsonage?' he said, echoing my question. 'You'll find 'en down that green lane, just past th'old school. But t'aint a parsonage nowadays. They've turned 'en into a guest house.' My next question stumped him. 'Thompson? Never heard o'no Thompson yereabouts.' Then he passed by, his cows tugging at the wayside grass.

I had inquired about Thompson because he was the centre of an eighteenth-century drama, the kind of thing that refutes what Stanley Baldwin called 'The stupid urban view of the countryside as dull ...' Thompson began his career by enlisting as a naval chaplain, a berth that enabled him to indulge in strong drink and other maritime habits. At the age of thirty-five he accepted the living of St Gennys, where he seems to have continued his heavy drinking. One night—perhaps after too much port—he not only dreamed of the last Judgement but also foresaw the precise hour at which he would be summoned thereto. As a result, he spent the next fortnight in his room, refusing to see anyone. During the third week he emerged, and informed his parishioners that within a few days he would die. At the appointed hour, in the company of two or three friends, he fell on his knees, awaiting the end. The clock struck; the hour passed; the man lived. But instead of exclaiming 'Therefore there is no God,' he passed the rest of his days as a zealous evangelical. In fact he became an admirer of John Wesley, accompanying him on his Cornish crusades, and inviting him to preach in St Gennys church. Thompson's flock however, did not approve their vicar's new style of oratory, which they described as 'circumferaneous vociferations'. The bishop was even more displeased. Indeed, he threatened to strip Thompson of his gown, whereupon the vicar replied by removing the gown himself, saying that he could preach just as well without it. He might have added that Wesley, an Anglican priest, was fully entitled to preach in St Gennys church. Years later, while staying at Camelford, Wesley made this entry in his *Journal*: 'Being informed that my old friend, Mr Thompson, Rector of St Gennys, was near death, and had expressed a desire to see me, I judged there was no time to be lost. So, borrowing the best horse I could find [Wesley was then in his eightieth year] I rode as fast as I could ... found Mr Thompson just alive ... He had many doubts concerning his final state, and rather feared, than desired to die; so that my whole business was to comfort him ... He desired me to administer the Lord's supper, which I willingly did; and I left him happier than I found him, calmly awaiting till his great change should come.' That was probably the most dramatic story ever to disturb this drowsy parish ... unless, of course, the smugglers arrived, pursued by Excisemen.

The coastal path lay a little more than a mile away, but to reach it proved difficult. As directed by the cowman, I passed the superannuated school, reflecting that times had changed since the children of St Gennys were educated, employed, and ultimately buried in the parish where they were born. Nowadays a bus collects them from their door or at a nearby crossroads, and away they go, from intimacy and agriculture, to a routine that will lead them into an office or a factory. Meanwhile, after perhaps three hundred yards, the track passed the old parsonage (in Wesley's day it may have been a rectory). Then came a narrow valley whose far side climbed to the clifftop. The going was now pleasant enough until, at the foot of the cliff, the dog and I had to guess our way through briars and swamp. After much scrambling we stood on the cliff, looking out to sea, man's first element, whence some humble creature reached the shore, there to crawl and to fly and to walk. Man himself is born with vestiges of a fish's gills; and if he is born a Briton of the old stock, then the brine is in his blood because, as Thomas Campbell stated, his ancestors ruled the waves:

> The spirit of your fathers
> Shall start from every wave,
> For the deck it was their field of fame,
> And Ocean was their grave.

Why were these waters called Atlantic? The answer lies with Atlas, a Greek God, who, it was believed, supported the pillars that supported the universe. Atlas was also the name of a Libyan mountain, likewise supposed to support the universe. Since Libya lay in Africa, the name Atlas was given to the sea along Africa's western coast, and finally to the entire expanse of water between Africa and America. Many times I had walked this coast while a gale bent me back as

I leaned into it; but now the air was as calm and warm as in
June. Even so, the coastline wore a white necklace, for the
Atlantic is never still. Wind or no wind, the rollers arrive,
breaking against the landfall. Turning north, I faced a stiff
climb, with a narrow spit of land on the left, which soon
rose high enough to hide the sea. Looking south, I saw the
valley and the tower of St Gennys church, four hundred feet
above the waves. The track then veered inland for a while,
but soon returned to the clifftop, so that I walked between
the Atlantic on one side and a panorama of bare hills on the
other. The map showed prehistoric tumuli within a short distance of the route. About the year 7000 BC a race of Middle
Stone Age people reached these parts, having crossed the
North Sea in three-log canoes. Some of their microliths or
small flint tools were found near Land's End. We owe much
to the makers of those primitive implements, without which
we might never have achieved anything more comfortable
than a sledge, or a cave, or a diet of berries and rhinoceros.
The Stone Age, therefore, was not a period of stagnation. It
witnessed man's fumbling experiments with movement and
materials and speech. Many centuries later, Cornwall was
occupied by a dark-haired people from the Mediterranean,
known as the Windmill People after one of their hilltop
camps near Avebury in Wiltshire. So the procession of immigrants advanced, bringing the Beaker Folk of the Bronze
Age. This Celtic legacy was recognized by the Saxon name
for Cornishmen, Cornwealas or 'Welshman in Cornwall'
(*Corn* being a form of *Cornovii*, a tribe of British Celts).
Like the Romans before them, neither the Saxons nor the
Normans attempted to colonize such a wild and remote
peninsula. During part of the Middle Ages the county had
no bishopric of its own, but lay within the diocese of Exeter,
some of whose prelates refused to risk life and limb by venturing westward from Plymouth. A semblance of that isola-
tion lingered until the beginning of the twentieth century,
allowing some parts of Cornwall to remain (in Edmund
Blunden's phrase) 'a modern Arcadia, just beyond the rail-

road ...' Holidaymakers, or settlers from across the Tamar, were called 'foreigners'.

Another reason for Cornwall's independence was its dearth of territorial noblemen, a class who, from their base at Court, did much to Londonize the less distant counties. The Cornish aristocracy was relatively small. During the reign of Elizabeth I no member of it resided permanently in the county. The real leaders were the gentry, most of whom stayed at home, and were related to one another. 'All Cornish gentlemen,' says the old maxim, 'are cousins.' Godolphins of Godolphin, Vyvyans of Trelowarren, Bassets of Tudy, St Aubyns of Clowance, Killigrews of Arwennack, Trevanions of Carhays, Treffrys of Fowey, Trelawneys of Trelawnce, Eliots of Port Eliot, Carews of Anthony, Edgcumbes of Cothele and Edgcumbe Mount ... such were the families whom Cobbett admired when he cited 'the difference between a resident *native* gentry, attached to the soil, known to every farmer and labourer from their childhood, frequently mixing with them in those pursuits where all artificial distinctions are lost, practising hospitality without ceremony ... and a gentry only now-and-then resident at all, having no relish for country-delights ... looking to the soil only for its rents ...'

The path was now so close to the cliffs that I could hear the boom of breakers below, but the sea itself was empty of shipping. Few vessels now visit the little harbours which during my childhood plied a brisk coastal trade from Newlyn north to Watchet. The famous Cornish fishing fleet has been overwhelmed by foreign competition and the cost of fuelling. Yet as recently as 1927 a guidebook mentioned 'the most characteristic of Cornish fishing methods ... the seine ... a huge wall of netting, with buoys at the surface and weights beneath; this is dipped where the fish are drawn out with a tuck net'. The chief catch was pilchards, which the Bretons called *sardines*. Quiller-Couch described the plight of Cornwall at the turn of the century: 'I see Cornwall impoverished by the evil days on which mining and (to a less degree) agriculture have fallen ...' Between 1924 and 1950 the number of Cornish fishing boats dropped from 953 to 420; the number of Cornish fishermen, from 3,110 to 820. Thereafter the decline grew swifter and steeper. In 1976 several Cornish 'fishing villages' lacked a single native who lived solely by fishing. Yet those same villages contain one or two veterans who can remember the heydays of Cornish fishing, as described by Francis Kilvert: 'The Vicar of St Ives says the smell of fish there is sometimes so terrific as to stop the church clock.' Fishing and farming and mining were the three great industries, the bread and butter, of Victorian Cornwall. Even in 1972, when the county had long since succumbed to tourism, a Cornish poet, J. C. Trewin, cited the old industries in his *Cornish Carol*:

> Tin we give 'ee from the mine,
> Barley-bread for harvest-sign,
> Fish that in the trawl-net shine ...

Sometimes the land on my left hid the sea; at other times it revealed a green-topped coastline curving south-west to Boscastle, and north beyond the garish caravan sites at Widemouth Bay. This coast was long ago called Sailor's Graveyard. At Morwenstow, the county's most northerly parish, one of the Victorian vicars, R. S. Hawker, reserved part of his churchyard for the burial of people who had been washed ashore from wrecks. The Cornish themselves earned an evil reputation as looters who were not unwilling to lure a ship onto the rocks by flashing deceptive lanterns. In 1611, when Sir John Killigrew built a lighthouse at Land's End, the local men protested that he was depriving them of a source of livelihood. In 1753 George Borlase deplored the misconduct of his fellow-Cornishmen: 'The people who make it their business to attend these wrecks are generally Tyners and, as soon as they observe a ship on the coast, they first arm themselves with sharp axes and hatchetts and leave their tyn works to follow these ships ... I have seen many a poor man, half-dead, cast ashore and crawling out of reach of the waves, fallen upon and in a manner stripped naked by these villains . . .' Wesley, too, spoke out against 'that scandal of Cornwall, the plundering of wrecks'.

Despite the sunshine and the scenery, the green road was deserted. Holidaymakers evidently preferred the commercial beaches. So, I proceeded alone, more often climbing than descending. The landscape was very different from the lush combes and wooded hills of south Cornwall's Roseland, where a *ros* or 'wild country' escaped the rigours of Atlantic gales. The cliffs above St Gennys were treeless, and so also were many of the hills beyond. Few people ever had followed this route until smuggling became an industry during the eighteenth century, when heavy duties were levied on tea, brandy, silk, tobacco, and other luxuries. The industry reached its zenith when England imposed a continental blockade during the war with France. Like highwaymen, the smugglers were criminals, willing to murder and maim their victims. Large numbers of the population—rich and poor alike—shared the swag. In Norfolk, for example, Parson Woodforde, a devout and kindly man, wrote in his diary for 29 March 1777: 'Andrews the smuggler brought me this night about 1 o'clock a bagg of Hysop Tea . . .' The first line of defence against smugglers was a fleet of fast Revenue cutters. In 1784 eleven such ships patrolled the coast of Devon and Cornwall. In 1815 the government recruited ex-soldiers of the Napoleonic war, to serve as Riding Officers and foot patrols. These were the men who first linked the coastal paths into a more or less continuous route. Contrary to common belief, a coastal footpath is not public property. The right to walk along it was either granted by landowners or given to a private body such as the National Trust. This sector of the green road was given to the Trust by Wing-Commander A. G. Parnall, RAF, in memory of his brother and of all other aircrews who died defending Britain against Hitler.

The track was now so steep that I plodded on with head bent. When at last the strain on my legs slackened, I looked up and found that I had almost reached the summit. Clearer than ever, the coast curved fore-and-aft; green on top, golden below, edged with the blue sea's white waves. Tremoutha Haven was there, and High Cliff, the tallest in Cornwall, 731 feet above the Atlantic. Round the furthest westerly point stood Beeny Cliff, made famous by a Dorset stonemason's son who once walked this way, courting

> A very West-of-Wessex girl,
> As blithe as blithe could be.

The wooer was Thomas Hardy, at that time an architect's apprentice; the 'West-of-Wessex girl' was Emma Lavinia Gifford, sister of the rector of St Juliot, only a few miles from where I stood. Hardy went there to restore a church whose bench-ends were rotten, whose roof was infested with bats, and whose tower was so unsafe that the bells had been removed from it, and were lying on the floor of the transept. Miss Gifford, who happened to be staying at the rectory when Hardy arrived, described their first meeting: 'The front door bell rang, and the architect was ushered in. I had to receive him alone ... I was immediately arrested by his familiar appearance, as if I had seen him in a dream.' Without knowing so, the hostess foresaw the visitor's fame: 'I noticed a slip of blue paper sticking out of his pocket ... the blue paper proved to be the MS of a poem, and not a plan of the church ...' However, the church still contains one of Hardy's architectural sketches. The young couple soon afterwards married, not happily, for Mrs Hardy never came to terms with her husband's humble origins and profound pessimism. After all, it was scarcely flattering to be the wife of a man whose books revealed that he wished to die, but was afraid to kill himself. In the end, Emma Hardy suffered a severe mental breakdown. Hardy himself had already romanticized certain aspects of their courtship in a novel, *A Pair of Blue Eyes*, where Boscastle appears as Castle Bottrel. When his wife died he continued to romanticize their relationship despite an admission of 'the differences between us'. He looked back at St Juliot through rose-tinted spectacles and with a sense of remorse, evoking a bitter-sweet memory.

The older he grew, the fonder he became, in both meanings of that adjective. In fact, he composed a sequence of elegiac poems, with these cliffs as their setting:

> I found her out there
> On a slope few see,
> That falls westwardly
> To the salt-edged air . . .

Shortly before he died, Hardy returned to St Juliot, and wrote a poem, *Beeny Cliff*:

O the opal and the sapphire of that wandering westward sea,
And the woman riding high above with bright hair flapping
free . . .

It was his last visit to the scene of a dead idyll,

> for my sand is sinking,
> And I shall traverse love's old domain
> Never again.

From those sad associations I turned north, scanning the coast that zig-zagged to Morwenstow, the parish of Robert Stephen Hawker, who there held the first of what we now call Harvest Festivals. He decorated his church with wayside flowers, and baked the sacramental bread from corn which had been grown in his parish. Before Hawker died, in 1875, the festival had spread throughout England.

From Morwenstow I turned to the immediate prospect, which was daunting as well as dramatic. Hundreds of feet below, the rollers lunged leisurely onto a stony cove. Far above—higher than anything I yet encountered—I saw the cliff and the path. But how to reach them? The map showed a green path, but the cliff showed only bare rock. Very cautiously I descended, and at last found a narrow track, bisected by a stream flowing down from the long valley on my right. Here, surely, was a place where smugglers had met, not in brilliant sunshine, but on moonless nights, searching the darkness for the outlines of a ship, or flashing a lantern, or listening for the splash of muffled oars. The usual procedure was as follows: the contraband cargoes were rowed ashore, to be met by armed accomplices (those who carried only a cudgel were called batmen). While the oarsmen returned to their ship, the shore party loaded the tubs onto ponies and sometimes onto men (the so-called tubmen). And away they went, along the cliff or into the valley, terrifying those whom they could not corrupt. Each man might expect to receive one shilling for a night's work, plus five shillings if the run proceeded smoothly. This procedure, however, became very hazardous during the 1830s, when the coastal blockade was superseded by an efficient land force, the Preventative Water-Guard, forerunner of the modern Coastguard Service. In 1856 the control of the Water-Guard passed from the Customs authorities to the Admiralty, with whom it remained until 1925 and thereafter throughout the Second World War. The smugglers tried to defeat the new Water-Guard by changing their tactics. Instead of landing her contraband, a vessel would anchor it just below the surface. Next night the booty was retrieved by local men. The vessels were guided by a 'flasher' on shore, using a lantern whose beams could be directed with great accuracy. If a vessel decided to risk a daylight run, the local fishermen signalled 'All Clear' by handling their sails in a prearranged manner.

Meanwhile, I had first to leap the stream, which I did, and then to climb the bare rock, which I did. This was the hardest of all my journeys along the green roads; steeper than the ascent to Middle Knuck Farm on Offa's Dyke, and rougher than the scramble to the summit of the Sugarloaf Mountain in Monmouthshire. Sometimes I crawled on all fours. A few tufts of grass did show among the boulders, but chiefly I steered by glancing upward in search of a way between the rocks. At the halfway mark I rested, wondering whether a chance-in-a-million would reveal a chough, a breed once so common that Gilbert White watched them near Stane Street in Sussex. On this coast they were called Cornish choughs.

Ten years earlier, I had seen one in Pembrokeshire, gliding among up-draughts at the edge of the cliff and then rolling over on its back, uttering the 'ker-chuff' which gave it an onomatopoeic name. No chough appeared, however, though I swept the scene through glasses. What I did see was a buzzard, a predator so keen-eyed that it could spot a beetle far below, and so sharp-clawed that it could kill a rabbit.

The second half of the ascent was even tougher than the first. During one of several halts, I took off a metaphorical hat to the man whom Francis Kilvert mentioned in his diary for 1871: 'He told me he had once been up Cader Idris 4 times in one day for a £10 wager ...' Still, the view two-thirds of the way up justified the effort. Seaward and far below, the breakers rolled and unrolled like a white mat on the doorstep of England. Sky and water were of an equal blue, and one ship appeared, a small coaster, standing several miles out. The sight of her smoke reminded me of two facts: first, that radar and engine-rooms still give this coast a wide berth; second, that the green road did not become obsolete when smuggling was suppressed. On the contrary, the suppression enabled the coastguards to specialize in their present task, the surveillance of shipping. This they did by patrolling the coast, keeping so close to the edge that they could overlook every chasm or cove, no matter how small or indented. Encouraged by the coastguards' example, Cornishmen soon redeemed their evil reputation as wreckers; and never more gallantly than when HMS *Anson* was driven onto the rocks with the loss of more than one hundred lives. Although the warship struck only a few yards offshore, the waves formed a wall of foam between the crew and the beach. Through that wall several Cornishmen waded out, and were able to rescue some of the struggling survivors. Among those who watched the disaster was a Cornish cabinet-maker, Henry Trengrouse. Appalled by what he had seen, Trengrouse dedicated the rest of his life to inventing and improving a rocket that fired a line from shore to ship. The Admiralty gave him £50; the Royal Society of Arts gave him thirty guineas and a silver medal; the Tsar of Russia gave him a diamond ring. And that was about all. After a lifetime's work, Trengrouse died in obscurity. But during the half-century following his death, his inventions saved more than twelve thousand lives.

When at last I reached the top of the cliff, I looked down dizzily at the tufts of grass among the rocks. It was like standing on the ramparts of a ruined castle, raised perhaps by King Arthur, the foremost heroic figure of the Dark Ages. At Tintagel, they say, he built a castle; at Castel-an-Dinas he built a hunting lodge; on Bodmin Moor he built a Hall; and as he lay dying, he ordered his sword, Excalibur, to be cast into Dozmary Pool. So great was Arthur's fame that it inspired not only the French Vulgate Cycle of Romance but also the English Arthurian poets from Malory to Masefield. Milton came close to choosing Arthur as the hero of an epic poem, but in the end preferred Satan. Tennyson did choose Arthur, and predicted that he would come again, once more the leader of a nation in distress:

> He passes to be King among the dead.
> And after healing of his grievous wound,
> He comes again . . .

Did he ever exist? No one knows. Until quite recent times it was not considered respectable to take Arthur seriously, except as the hero of a fairy tale. Yet there is evidence to suggest that a great soldier did arise in those years, and did for a while unite a large number of British Celts. The legend of King Arthur was popularized by a twelfth-century bishop, Geoffrey of Monmouth, who claimed to have found the stories in a book (whose name he did not remember) written by a friend (whose surname he had forgotten). Much of Geoffrey's narrative is absurd, not least his claim that Arthur conquered the whole of Wales and France, and after them the Kings of Babylon, Egypt, Parthia, and Greece. Neverthe-less, the Middle Ages continued to hail Arthur as 'The once-and-always King' (*Rex quondam et futurus*) and as 'The

Flower of Kings' (*Flos Regum Arturus*). Most historians now agree that there may be some truth in some of the traditional tales about a soldier-king who led the Britons to victory over the Saxons at the Badonic Hill. As Masefield remarked, rather optimistically,

> All Britons know the stories that are told
> Of Arthur's battle ...

It is possible, and by some scholars is considered probable, that the Arthurian legends did not arise and flourish without some foundation in fact. The tall stories about Robin Hood and Hereward the Wake can be dismissed; but the existence of someone who really did lead a guerrilla army in Sherwood Forest or among the Fenland swamps cannot be dismissed until it has been proved false.

I had now reached the peak of my journey. The path kept so close to the edge of the cliff that barbed wire was set there, for the benefit of people who cannot see danger when they stare at it. The turf felt warm, and for the last of several times I sprang to defend the British climate. Tacitus, who never visited Britain, announced that it was a fog-ridden island (a piece of misinformation which he acquired from his father-in-law, governor of Britain). Caesar, who visited the island twice, gave an accurate report of conditions in the southern parts : 'The climate is more temperate than Gaul, and the frost less severe.' Nevertheless, the false rumours continued to circulate. Victor Hugo, who ought to have known better, complained that the British sun was as chilly as the moon (*ressemble à la lune*). Yet only once, in winter, had bad weather defeated my journeys along the green roads of Britain; and never at all had it failed to produce a few rays of sunshine. On most occasions, you remember, it produced a day out of the blue, the blue sky. This day, certainly, was no Keatsian September of mists. It was sheer summer, tinged with the zest of spring. Time after time I halted, staring at the sea and then at the distant blotch of caravans and hotels and bungalows and car parks. Undismayed by those blemishes, the Atlantic obeyed Byron's command:

> Roll on, thou deep and dark blue Ocean—roll!
> Ten thousand fleets sweep over thee in vain;
> Man marks the earth with ruin—his control
> Stops with the shore.

Beside the cliff pathway I noticed a boulder with six words painted on it: *Agan Tas, neb us yn nef.* These I copied down for future reference, bearing in mind that *yn* was a Celtic word, and that a quaint clique were trying to achieve the impossible by restoring a dead language to life. Investigation showed that the six words were part of the Cornish paternoster: *bydhens uchellyns dhe hanow, dens dhe wlascor, dhe vodh re be gwreys yn nor cepay hag yn nef.* Those tongue-twisters from the Brythonic branch of the Celtic language were spoken throughout Cornwall and in parts of Devon until the end of the Middle Ages. The first five Cornish numerals were *un, deu, try, peswar, pemp*; of which the first three are recognizable as the French *un, deux, trois*; while the last recalls the Greek *pente*. As late as 1549 the Cornish language was lively enough to incite a rebellion when London imposed an English Bible and Prayer Book on Cornwall. Forty years later, however, John Norden noticed a decline, comparable with Boswell's obituary of the Gaelic in Scotland: 'Of late,' wrote Norden, 'the Cornish men have much conformed themselves to the use of the English tongue ... especially in the eastern parties.' It was the familiar story of a culture that died with its language. Even so, in 1640 the vicar of St Feock was still administering the Sacrament in Cornish; and nearly half a century later the vicar of Landewenack preached the last Cornish sermon of which we possess record. Even in 1777 Dolly Pentreath was speaking the old language. An inscription on her tomb at Paul, near Penzance, claims that she was the last person who spoke it fluently. The tomb itself was paid for by Lucien Bonaparte, an amateur philologist, who seems to have been misled by the local people, because the church-yard at Zennor contains a memorial to John Davey, claim-ing that he was speaking Cornish during the 1890s. A langu-age, of course, does not necessarily die when it ceases to be spoken. Only a very few scholars can now speak Latin and classical Greek, yet those languages live in their influence on European literature and civilization. Many of Cromwell's foreign despatches were translated into Latin by John Milton. Latin, indeed, remained the official language of Hungarian diplomacy until 1848; and it still forms part of the language of lawyers, doctors, and botanists. Cornish, on the other hand, really is dead. Moreover, its scanty literature—a handful of biographies and plays—seems a poor reward for mastering a tongue that will never be spoken except by a few Celto-philes at Cornish rallies and cultural coffee mornings. Sir Arthur Quiller-Couch was Cornish to the marrow (or very nearly so, his mother being a Devonian), yet he ridiculed the zealots who make believe that the Cornish language can be revived, either as a medium of literature or as a means of communication in the affairs of daily life. Although he was an Oxford graduate and a Cambridge professor, Q him-self fell from grace when he coined the phrase 'Delectable Duchy' as a synonym for Cornwall. As we observed on the Abbot's Way, the Duchy of Cornwall includes a large part of Devon.

I had expected to meet other walkers along this road, but my expectation was unfulfilled. Never before on my chosen journeys had I travelled in such solitude so close to such crowds. I could see them through glasses, herding like a flock of sheep. The prehistoric Celts would have been amazed by the modern Englishman's passion for not being alone. They kept to themselves, living for the most part in *trefs* or small communities. Mechanized man, by contrast, seems to enjoy living close-packed among bricks and mortar and con-crete. The multiplicity of Cornish *trefs* can be gauged by the number of them that survive as place-names: Tregnaer ('hamlet near a *caer* or fort'), Tregarn ('hamlet with a *carn* or rock'), Tremaine ('hamlet near a *maen* or stone'), Trenglos ('hamlet with an *eglos* or church'). The last example shows the affinity between Cornish, Welsh, and the ancient Gallic speech, because 'church' is *eglws* in Welsh and *église* in French. At the beginning of the twentieth century the United Kingdom employed six languages for everyday use or on formal civic occasions; namely, English, Welsh, Erse, Gaelic, Manx, and several variations of Norman–French; to which was added the study of the Cornish language.

As once before on my journeys, the scene came suddenly and unexpectedly to life; not so vividly as along the Scottish drove road, yet sufficient to re-create something of a populous past. Two more ships appeared, all standing well out, all heading north-east towards the Severn Sea and thence perhaps to Bristol or one of the Welsh ports. Then, from the opposite direction, making for the Atlantic, a small warship appeared, her bow ploughing a creamy furrow; her White Ensign taut on the breeze. Was it not strange, I thought, that, in an increasingly hostile world, this island continued to whittle away the first and last defence of its own lifelines, and to squander money on things which would disappear if ever those lifelines failed? Though Heaven might hear them, the crew of that small and overworked warship received but a dusty answer when they appealed to their fellow countrymen 'that we may be ... a security for such as pass on the seas upon their lawful occasions; that the inhabitants of our Island may in peace and quietness ...' Three centuries ago the Marquess of Halifax composed *A Draft of a New Model at Sea*, in which he uttered a warning : 'It may now be said to England, "Martha, Martha, thou art busy about many things, but one thing is necessary. To the question, What shall we do to be saved in this World? There is but one answer but this; Look to your Moat."' England, the Marquess insisted, is an island; therefore 'The first Article in an Englishman's Political Creed must be, That he believeth in the Sea ...' No new weapon, no new alliance— not even the latest Utopian daydream—have outdated those words. We are an island still, and over the sea comes the bulk of our material nourishment.

Having no wish to descend the rocky pathway which I had lately climbed, I decided to call it a day while the sun was still warm. A footpath on the right would lead me to a lane that joined the main road a few miles inland. I took a last look at the Atlantic, as calm and as blue as at noon. Yet tomorrow, if the wind shifted, that same Ocean would raise the ghosts of Swinburne's schooners listening anxiously

> To the loud rocks and surging reaches home
> That take the wild wrath of the Cornish foam.

It was inevitable that I should feel elegiac while the footpath beckoned me from a westering sun. In one way and another—walking, reading, writing—the task of describing some of the green roads of Britain had occupied me for three years, and was in a sense the harvest of a lifetime's activity. As I walked the last yards of the last journey, I asked myself which among the roads had given me the greatest pleasure. There ought to have been only one answer, yet I found nine. I loved best the Icknield Way because I had known it for nearly forty years. The road that I remembered most vividly was Offa's Dyke, partly on account of my companions there, and partly on account of the weather, which out-topped perfection. For sheer grandeur I chose the view from Sugarloaf Mountain in Monmouthshire; for historic associations, Stane Street; for beauty, the last serene lap of the Kennet and Avon Canal; for spaciousness, the Scottish drove road; for lightheartedness, the Inkpen Beacon (despite The Thing); for ruggedness, the Abbot's Way; for the sea, the North Cornish coast.

So, in the end, each road had offered its own excellence, and all had revealed certain traits—both of people and of places—which suggested that Britain, though no longer Great, might still by her own exertions remain for the most part a green and pleasant land.

Index